Mastering Python Forensics

Master the art of digital forensics and analysis
with Python

Dr. Michael Spreitzenbarth

Dr. Johann Uhrmann

BIRMINGHAM - MUMBAI

Mastering Python Forensics

First published: October 2015

Production reference: 1261015

Published by Packt Publishing Ltd.
Livery Place
35 Livery Street
Birmingham B3 2PB, UK.

ISBN 978-1-78398-804-4

www.packtpub.com

Credits

Authors
Dr. Michael Spreitzenbarth
Dr. Johann Uhrmann

Reviewers
Richard Marsden
Puneet Narula
Yves Vandermeer

Commissioning Editor
Kartikey Pandey

Acquisition Editor
Sonali Vernekar

Content Development Editor
Shweta Pant

Technical Editor
Pranil Pathare

Copy Editor
Vibha Shukla

Project Coordinator
Shipra Chawhan

Proofreader
Safis Editing

Indexer
Mariammal Chettiyar

Production Coordinator
Arvindkumar Gupta

Cover Work
Arvindkumar Gupta

About the Authors

Dr. Michael Spreitzenbarth holds a degree of doctor of engineering in IT security from the University of Erlangen-Nuremberg and is a CISSP as well as a GMOB. He has been an IT security consultant at a worldwide operating CERT for more than three years and has worked as a freelancer in the field of mobile phone forensics, malware analysis, and IT security consultancy for more than six years. Since the last four years, he has been giving talks and lectures in the fields of forensics and mobile security at various universities and in the private sector.

I would like to thank everyone who has encouraged me while writing this book, especially my wife for her great support. I would also like to thank all the authors of the used open source tools— without your help, this book wouldn't have been possible.

Dr. Johann Uhrmann holds a degree in computer science from the University of Applied Sciences Landshut and a doctor of engineering from the University of the German Federal Armed Forces. He has more than ten years of experience in software development, which includes working for start-ups, institutional research, and corporate environment. Johann has several years of experience in incident handling and IT governance, focusing on Linux and Cloud environments.

First of all, I would like to thank my wife, Daniela, for her moral support and willingness to give up on some family time while I was writing. I also would like to thank my coauthor and colleague, Dr. Michael Spreitzenbarth, for talking me into writing this book and handling a great deal of the organizational overhead of such a project. Furthermore, the great people working on all the open source software projects that we used and mentioned in this book deserve credit. You are the guys who keep the IT world spinning.

About the Reviewers

Richard Marsden has over twenty years of professional experience in software development. After starting in the fields of geophysics and oil exploration, he has spent the last twelve years running the Winwaed Software Technology LLC, an independent software vendor. Winwaed specializes in geospatial tools and applications, which include web applications, and operates the `http://www.mapping-tools.com` website for tools and add-ins for geospatial products, such as Caliper's Maptitude and Microsoft's MapPoint.

Richard was also a technical reviewer for *Python Geospatial Development*, and *Python Geospatial Analysis Essentials*, both written by *Erik Westra, Packt Publishing*.

Puneet Narula is currently working as PPC Data Analyst with Hostelworld.com Ltd (`http://www.hostelworld.com/`), Dublin, Ireland, where he analyzes massive clickstream data from direct and affiliate sources and provides insight to the digital marketing team. He uses RapidMiner, R, and Python for the exploratory and predictive analysis. His areas of expertise are programming in Python and R, machine learning, data analysis and Tableau.

He started his career in banking and finance and then moved to the ever growing domain of data and analytics.

He earned MSc in computing (data analytics) from Dublin Institute of Technology, Dublin, Ireland. He has reviewed the books: *Python Data Analysis*, by *Ivan Idris, Packt Publishing* and *Python Geospatial Analysis Essentials*, by *Erik Westra, Packt Publishing*.

Yves Vandermeer is a police officer working for the Belgian Federal Police. He has been involved in major investigations since 1997, where he contributed to recovering digital evidence. Owning a MSc in computer forensics, Yves is also a trainer on several topics such as filesystems and network forensics for several law enforcement agencies.

Chairing the European Cybercrime Training and Education Group, E.C.T.E.G., since 2013, Yves supports the creation of training materials that are focused on the understanding of the concepts applied in practical exercises.

Using his experience, he developed forensic software tools for law enforcement and contributed to several advisory groups related to IT crime and IT forensics.

www.PacktPub.com

Support files, eBooks, discount offers, and more

For support files and downloads related to your book, please visit www.PacktPub.com.

Did you know that Packt offers eBook versions of every book published, with PDF and ePub files available? You can upgrade to the eBook version at www.PacktPub.com and as a print book customer, you are entitled to a discount on the eBook copy. Get in touch with us at service@packtpub.com for more details.

At www.PacktPub.com, you can also read a collection of free technical articles, sign up for a range of free newsletters and receive exclusive discounts and offers on Packt books and eBooks.

https://www2.packtpub.com/books/subscription/packtlib

Do you need instant solutions to your IT questions? PacktLib is Packt's online digital book library. Here, you can search, access, and read Packt's entire library of books.

Why subscribe?

- Fully searchable across every book published by Packt
- Copy and paste, print, and bookmark content
- On demand and accessible via a web browser

Free access for Packt account holders

If you have an account with Packt at www.PacktPub.com, you can use this to access PacktLib today and view 9 entirely free books. Simply use your login credentials for immediate access.

Table of Contents

Preface

Today, information technology is a part of almost everything that surrounds us. These are the systems that we wear and that support us in building and running cities, companies, our personal online shopping tours, and our friendships. These systems are attractive to use—and abuse. Consequently, all criminal fields such as theft, fraud, blackmailing, and so on expanded to the IT. Nowadays, this is a multi-billion, criminal, global shadow industry.

Can a single person spot traces of criminal or suspicious activity conducted by a multi-billion, criminal, global shadow industry? Well, sometimes you can. To analyze the modern crime, you do not need magnifying glasses and lifting fingerprints off wine bottles. Instead, we will see how to apply your Python skills to get a close look at the most promising spots on a file system and take digital fingerprints from the traces left behind by hackers.

As authors, we believe in the strength of examples over dusty theory. This is why we provide samples for forensic tooling and scripts, which are short enough to be understood by the average Python programmer, yet usable tools and building blocks for real-world IT forensics.

Are you ready to turn *suspicion* into hard facts?

What this book covers

Chapter 1, Setting Up the Lab and Introduction to Python ctypes, covers how to set up your environment to follow the examples that are provided in this book. We will take a look at the various Python modules that support our forensic analyses. With ctypes, we provide the means to go beyond Python modules and leverage the capabilities of native system libraries.

Chapter 2, Forensic Algorithms, provides you with the digital equivalent of taking fingerprints. Just like in the case of classic fingerprints, we will show you how to compare the digital fingerprints with a huge registry of the known good and bad samples. This will support you in focusing your analysis and providing a proof of forensical soundness.

Chapter 3, Using Python for Windows and Linux Forensics, is the first step on your journey to understanding digital evidence. We will provide examples to detect signs of compromise on Windows and Linux systems. We will conclude the chapter with an example on how to use machine learning algorithms in the forensic analysis.

Chapter 4, Using Python for Network Forensics, is all about capturing and analyzing network traffic. With the provided tools, you can search and analyze the network traffic for signs of exfiltration or signature of malware communication.

Chapter 5, Using Python for Virtualization Forensics, explains how modern virtualization concepts can be used by the attacker and forensic analyst. Consequently, we will show how to find traces of malicious behavior on the hypervisor level and utilize the virtualization layer as a reliable source of forensic data.

Chapter 6, Using Python for Mobile Forensics, will give you an insight on how to retrieve and analyze forensic data from mobile devices. The examples will include analyzing Android devices as well as Apple iOS devices.

Chapter 7, Using Python for Memory Forensics, demonstrates how to retrieve memory snapshots and analyze these RAM images forensically with Linux and Android. With the help of tools such as LiME and Volatility, we will demonstrate how to extract information from the system memory.

What you need for this book

All you need for this book is a Linux workstation with a Python 2.7 environment and a working Internet connection. *Chapter 1, Setting Up the Lab and Introduction to Python ctypes,* will guide you through the installation of the additional Python modules and tools. All of our used tools are freely available from the Internet. The source code of our samples is available from Packt Publishing.

To follow the examples of *Chapter 5, Using Python for Virtualization Forensics,* you may want to set up a virtualization environment with VMware vSphere. The required software is available from VMware as time-limited trial version without any functional constraints.

While not strictly required, we recommend trying some of the examples of *Chapter 6, Using Python for Mobile Forensics*, on discarded mobile devices. For your first experiments, please refrain from using personal or business phones that are actually in use.

Who this book is for

This book is for IT administrators, IT operations, and analysts who want to gain profound skills in the collection and analysis of digital evidence. If you are already a forensic expert, this book will help you to expand your knowledge in new areas such as virtualization or mobile devices.

To get the most out of this book, you should have decent skills in Python and understand at least some inner workings of your forensic targets. For example, some file system details.

Conventions

In this book, you will find a number of text styles that distinguish between different kinds of information. Here are some examples of these styles and an explanation of their meaning.

Code words in text, database table names, folder names, filenames, file extensions, pathnames, dummy URLs, user input, and Twitter handles are shown as follows: "Note that in the case of Windows, `msvcrt` is the MS standard C library containing most of the standard C functions and uses the `cdecl` calling convention (on Linux systems, the similar library would be `libc.so.6`)."

A block of code is set as follows:

```
def multi_hash(filename):
    """Calculates the md5 and sha256 hashes
    of the specified file and returns a list
    containing the hash sums as hex strings."""
```

When we wish to draw your attention to a particular part of a code block, the relevant lines or items are set in bold:

```
<Event xmlns="http://schemas.microsoft.com/win/2004/08/events/
event"><System><Provider Name="Microsoft-Windows-Security-Auditing"
Guid="54849625-5478-4994-a5ba-3e3b0328c30d"></Provider>
<EventID Qualifiers="">4724</EventID>
<Version>0</Version>
<Level>0</Level>
<Task>13824</Task>
```

Any command-line input or output is written as follows:

```
user@lab:~$ virtualenv labenv
New python executable in labenv/bin/python
Installing setuptools, pip...done.
```

New terms and **important words** are shown in bold. Words that you see on the screen, for example, in menus or dialog boxes, appear in the text like this: "When asked to **Select System Logs**, ensure that all log types are selected."

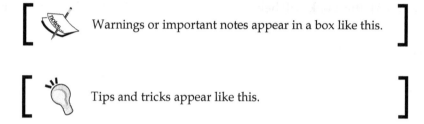

> Warnings or important notes appear in a box like this.

> Tips and tricks appear like this.

Reader feedback

Feedback from our readers is always welcome. Let us know what you think about this book—what you liked or disliked. Reader feedback is important for us as it helps us develop titles that you will really get the most out of.

To send us general feedback, simply e-mail feedback@packtpub.com, and mention the book's title in the subject of your message.

If there is a topic that you have expertise in and you are interested in either writing or contributing to a book, see our author guide at www.packtpub.com/authors.

Customer support

Now that you are the proud owner of a Packt book, we have a number of things to help you to get the most from your purchase.

Downloading the example code

You can download the example code files from your account at http://www.packtpub.com for all the Packt Publishing books you have purchased. If you purchased this book elsewhere, you can visit http://www.packtpub.com/support and register to have the files e-mailed directly to you.

Errata

Although we have taken every care to ensure the accuracy of our content, mistakes do happen. If you find a mistake in one of our books—maybe a mistake in the text or the code—we would be grateful if you could report this to us. By doing so, you can save other readers from frustration and help us improve subsequent versions of this book. If you find any errata, please report them by visiting http://www.packtpub.com/submit-errata, selecting your book, clicking on the **Errata Submission Form** link, and entering the details of your errata. Once your errata are verified, your submission will be accepted and the errata will be uploaded to our website or added to any list of existing errata under the Errata section of that title.

To view the previously submitted errata, go to https://www.packtpub.com/books/content/support and enter the name of the book in the search field. The required information will appear under the **Errata** section.

Piracy

Piracy of copyrighted material on the Internet is an ongoing problem across all media. At Packt, we take the protection of our copyright and licenses very seriously. If you come across any illegal copies of our works in any form on the Internet, please provide us with the location address or website name immediately so that we can pursue a remedy.

Please contact us at copyright@packtpub.com with a link to the suspected pirated material.

We appreciate your help in protecting our authors and our ability to bring you valuable content.

Questions

If you have a problem with any aspect of this book, you can contact us at questions@packtpub.com, and we will do our best to address the problem.

1

Setting Up the Lab and Introduction to Python ctypes

Cyber Security and **Digital Forensics** are two topics of increasing importance. Digital forensics especially, is getting more and more important, not only during law enforcement investigations, but also in the field of incident response. During all of the previously mentioned investigations, it's fundamental to get to know the root cause of a security breach, malfunction of a system, or a crime. Digital forensics plays a major role in overcoming these challenges.

In this book, we will teach you how to build your own lab and perform profound digital forensic investigations, which originate from a large range of platforms and systems, with the help of Python. We will start with common Windows and Linux desktop machines, then move forward to cloud and virtualization platforms, and end up with mobile phones. We will not only show you how to examine the data at rest or in transit, but also take a deeper look at the volatile memory.

Python provides an excellent development platform to build your own investigative tools because of its decreased complexity, increased efficiency, large number of third-party libraries, and it's also easy to read and write. During the journey of reading this book, you will not only learn how to use the most common Python libraries and extensions to analyze the evidence, but also how to write your own scripts and helper tools to work faster on the cases or incidents with a huge amount of evidence that has to be analyzed.

Let's begin our journey of mastering Python forensics by setting up our lab environment, followed by a brief introduction of the Python ctypes.

If you have already worked with Python **ctypes** and have a working lab environment, feel free to skip the first chapter and start directly with one of the other chapters. After the first chapter, the other chapters are fairly independent of each other and can be read in any order.

Setting up the Lab

As a base for our scripts and investigations, we need a comprehensive and powerful lab environment that is able to handle a large number of different file types and structures as well as connections to mobile devices. To achieve this goal, we will use the latest Ubuntu LTS version 14.04.2 and install it in a virtual machine (VM). Within the following sections, we will explain the setup of the VM and introduce Python **virtualenv**, which we will use to establish our working environment.

Ubuntu

To work in a similar lab environment, we suggest you to download a copy of the latest Ubuntu LTS Desktop Distribution from `http://www.ubuntu.com/download/desktop/`, preferably the 32-bit version. The distribution provides a simple-to-use UI and already has the Python 2.7.6 environment installed and preconfigured. Throughout the book, we will use Python 2.7.x and not the newer 3.x versions. Several examples and case studies in this book will rely on the tools or libraries that are already a part of the Ubuntu distribution. When a chapter or section of the book requires a third-party package or library, we will provide the additional information on how to install it in the **virtualenv** (the setup of this environment will be explained in the next section) or on Ubuntu in general.

For better performance of the system, we recommend that the virtual machine that is used for the lab has at least 4 GB of volatile memory and about 40 GB of storage.

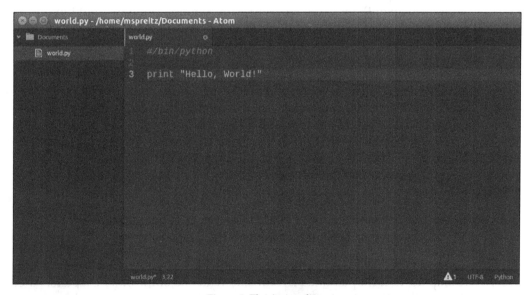

Figure 1: The Atom editor

To write your first Python script, you can use a simple editor such as **vi** or a powerful but cluttered IDE such as **eclipse**. As a really powerful alternative, we would suggest you to use **atom**, a very clean but highly customizable editor that can be freely downloaded from `https://atom.io/`.

Python virtual environment (virtualenv)

According to the official Python documentation, Virtual Environment is a tool to keep the dependencies required by different projects in separate places by creating virtual Python environments for them. It solves the "Project X depends on version 1.x, but Project Y needs 4.x" dilemma and keeps your global site-packages directory clean and manageable.

This is also what we will use in the following chapters to keep a common environment for all the readers of the book and not run into any compatibility issues. First of all, we have to install the **virtualenv** package. This is done by the following command:

```
user@lab:~$ pip install virtualenv
```

We will now create a folder in the users' home directory for our virtual Python environment. This directory will contain the executable Python files and a copy of the pip library, which can be used to install other packages in the environment. The name of the virtual environment (in our case, it is called **labenv**) can be of your choice. Our virtual lab environment can be created by executing the following command:

```
user@lab:~$ virtualenv labenv
New python executable in labenv/bin/python
Installing setuptools, pip...done.
```

To start working with the new lab environment, it first needs to be activated. This can be done through:

```
user@lab:~$ source labenv/bin/activate
(labenv)user@lab:~$
```

Now, you can see that the command prompt starts with the name of the virtual environment that we activated. From now on, any package that you install using pip will be placed in the **labenv** folder, isolated from the global Python installation in the underlying Ubuntu.

Throughout the book, we will use this virtual python environment and install new packages and libraries in it from time to time. So, every time you try to recap a shown example remember or challenge to change into the **labenv** environment before running your scripts.

If you are done working in the virtual environment for the moment and you want to return to your "normal" Python environment, you can deactivate the virtual environment by executing the following command:

```
(labenv)user@lab:~$ deactivate
user@lab:~$
```

This puts you back in the system's default Python interpreter with all its installed libraries and dependencies.

If you are using more than one virtual or physical machine for the investigations, the virtual environments can help you to keep your libraries and packages synced with all these workplaces. In order to ensure that your environments are consistent, it's a good idea to "freeze" the current state of environment packages. To do this, just run:

```
(labenv)user@lab:~$ pip freeze > requirenments.txt
```

This will create a `requirements.txt` file, which contains a simple list of all the packages in the current environment and their respective versions. If you want to now install the same packages using the same version on a different machine, just copy the `requirements.txt` file to the desired machine, create the **labenv** environment as described earlier and execute the following command:

```
(labenv)user@lab:~$ pip install -r requirements.txt
```

Now, you will have consistent Python environments on all the machines and don't need to worry about different library versions or other dependencies.

After we have created the Ubuntu virtual machine with our dedicated lab environment, we are nearly ready to start our first forensic analysis. But before that, we need more knowledge of the helpful Python libraries and backgrounds. Therefore, we will start with an introduction to the Python **ctypes** in the following section.

Introduction to Python ctypes

According to the official Python documentation, **ctypes** is a foreign function library that provides C compatible data types and allows calling functions in DLLs or shared libraries. A foreign function library means that the Python code can call C functions using only Python, without requiring special or custom-made extensions.

This module is one of the most powerful libraries available to the Python developer. The **ctypes** library enables you to not only call functions in dynamically linked libraries (as described earlier), but can also be used for low-level memory manipulation. It is important that you understand the basics of how to use the **ctypes** library as it will be used for many examples and real-world cases throughout the book.

In the following sections, we will introduce some basic features of Python **ctypes** and how to use them.

Working with Dynamic Link Libraries

Python **ctypes** export the `cdll` and on Windows `windll` or respectively `oledll` objects, to load the requested dynamic link libraries. A dynamically linked library is a compiled binary that is linked at runtime to the executable main process. On Windows platforms, these binaries are called **Dynamic Link Libraries** (DLL) and on Linux, they are called **shared objects** (SO). You can load these linked libraries by accessing them as the attributes of the `cdll`, `windll` or `oledll` objects. Now, we will demonstrate a very brief example for Windows and Linux to get the current time directly out of the `time` function in `libc` (this library defines the system calls and other basic facilities such as `open`, `printf`, or `exit`).

Note that in the case of Windows, `msvcrt` is the MS standard C library containing most of the standard C functions and uses the `cdecl` calling convention (on Linux systems, the similar library would be `libc.so.6`):

```
C:\Users\Admin>python

>>> from ctypes import *
>>> libc = cdll.msvcrt
>>> print libc.time(None)
1428180920
```

Windows appends the usual `.dll` file suffix automatically. On Linux, it is required to specify the filename, including the extension, to load the chosen library. Either the `LoadLibrary()` method of the DLL loaders should be used or you should load the library by creating an instance of `CDLL` by calling the constructor, as shown in the following code:

```
(labenv)user@lab:~$ python

>>> from ctypes import *
>>> libc = CDLL("libc.so.6")
>>> print libc.time(None)
1428180920
```

As shown in these two examples, it is very easy to be able to call to a dynamic library and use a function that is exported. You will be using this technique many times throughout the book, so it is important that you understand how it works.

C data types

When looking at the two examples from the earlier section in detail, you can see that we use None as one of the parameters for a dynamically linked C library. This is possible because None, integers, longs, byte strings, and unicode strings are the native Python objects that can be directly used as the parameters in these function calls. None is passed as a C, NULL pointer, byte strings, and unicode strings are passed as pointers to the memory block that contains their data (char * or wchar_t *). Python integers and Python longs are passed as the platform's default C int type, their value is masked to fit into the C type. A complete overview of the Python types and their corresponding ctype types can be seen in *Table 1*:

ctypes type	C type	Python type
c_bool (https://docs.python.org/2/library/ctypes.html#ctypes.c_bool)	_Bool	bool (1)
c_char (https://docs.python.org/2/library/ctypes.html#ctypes.c_char)	char	1-character string
c_wchar (https://docs.python.org/2/library/ctypes.html#ctypes.c_wchar)	wchar_t	1-character unicode string
c_byte (https://docs.python.org/2/library/ctypes.html#ctypes.c_byte)	char	int/long
c_ubyte (https://docs.python.org/2/library/ctypes.html#ctypes.c_ubyte)	unsigned char	int/long
c_short (https://docs.python.org/2/library/ctypes.html#ctypes.c_short)	short	int/long
c_ushort (https://docs.python.org/2/library/ctypes.html#ctypes.c_ushort)	unsigned short	int/long
c_int (https://docs.python.org/2/library/ctypes.html#ctypes.c_int)	int	int/long
c_uint (https://docs.python.org/2/library/ctypes.html#ctypes.c_uint)	unsigned int	int/long
c_long (https://docs.python.org/2/library/ctypes.html#ctypes.c_long)	long	int/long

ctypes type	C type	Python type
c_ulong (https://docs.python.org/2/library/ctypes.html#ctypes.c_ulong)	unsigned long	int/long
c_longlong (https://docs.python.org/2/library/ctypes.html#ctypes.c_longlong)	__int64 or long long	int/long
c_ulonglong (https://docs.python.org/2/library/ctypes.html#ctypes.c_ulonglong)	unsigned __int64 or unsigned long long	int/long
c_float (https://docs.python.org/2/library/ctypes.html#ctypes.c_float)	float	float
c_double (https://docs.python.org/2/library/ctypes.html#ctypes.c_double)	double	float
c_longdouble (https://docs.python.org/2/library/ctypes.html#ctypes.c_longdouble)	long double	float
c_char_p (https://docs.python.org/2/library/ctypes.html#ctypes.c_char_p)	char * (NUL terminated)	string or None
c_wchar_p (https://docs.python.org/2/library/ctypes.html#ctypes.c_wchar_p)	wchar_t * (NUL terminated)	unicode or None
c_void_p (https://docs.python.org/2/library/ctypes.html#ctypes.c_void_p)	void *	int/long or None

Table 1: Fundamental Data Types

This table is very helpful because all the Python types except `integers`, `strings`, and `unicode strings` have to be wrapped in their corresponding ctypes type so that they can be converted to the required C data type in the linked library and not throw the `TypeError` exceptions, as shown in the following code:

```
(labenv)user@lab:~$ python


>>> from ctypes import *
>>> libc = CDLL("libc.so.6")
>>> printf = libc.printf


>>> printf("An int %d, a double %f\n", 4711, 47.11)
```

```
Traceback (most recent call last):
  File "<stdin>", line 1, in <module>
ctypes.ArgumentError: argument 3: <type 'exceptions.TypeError'>: Don't
know how to convert parameter 3


>>> printf("An int %d, a double %f\n", 4711, c_double(47.11))
An int 4711, a double 47.110000
```

Defining Unions and Structures

Unions and **Structures** are important data types because they are frequently used throughout the `libc` on Linux and also in the Microsoft Win32 API.

Unions are simply a group of variables, which can be of the same or different data types, where all of its members share the same memory location. By storing variables in this way, unions allow you to specify the same value in different types. For the upcoming example, we will change from the interactive Python shell to the atom editor on our Ubuntu lab environment. You just need to open atom editor, type in the following code, and save it under the name `new_evidence.py`:

```
from ctypes import *

class case(Union):
        _fields_ = [
        ("evidence_int", c_int),
        ("evidence_long", c_long),
        ("evidence_char", c_char * 4)
        ]

value = raw_input("Enter new evidence number:")
new_evidence = case(int(value))
print "Evidence number as a int: %i" % new_evidence.evidence_int
print "Evidence number as a long: %ld" % new_evidence.evidence_long
print "Evidence number as a char: %s" % new_evidence.evidence_char
```

If you assign the `evidence` union's member variable `evidence_int` a value of `42`, you can then use the `evidence_char` member to display the character representation of that number, as shown in the following example:

```
(labenv)user@lab:~$ python new_evidence.py


Enter new evidence number:42


Evidence number as a long: 42
Evidence number as a int: 42
Evidence number as a char: *
```

As you can see in the preceding example, by assigning the union a single value, you get three different representations of that value. For `int` and `long`, the displayed output is obvious but for the `evidence_char` variable, it could be a bit confusing. In this case, `'*'` is the ASCII character with the value of the equivalent of decimal `42`. The `evidence_char` member variable is a good example of how to define an `array` in ctypes. In ctypes, an array is defined by multiplying a type by the number of elements that you want to allocate in the array. In this example, a four-element character array was defined for the member variable `evidence_char`.

A structure is very similar to unions, but the members do not share the same memory location. You can access any of the member variables in the structure using dot notation, such as `case.name`. This would access the `name` variable contained in the `case` structure. The following is a very brief example of how to create a `structure` (or **struct,** as they are often called) with three members: `name`, `number`, and `investigator_name` so that all can be accessed by the dot notation:

```
from ctypes import *

class case(Structure):
        _fields_ = [
        ("name", c_char * 16),
        ("number", c_int),
        ("investigator_name", c_char * 8)
        ]
```

Summary

In the first chapter, we created our lab environment: a virtual machine running **Ubuntu 14.04.2 LTS**. This step is really important as you can now create snapshots before working on real evidence and are able to roll back to a clean machine state after finishing the investigation. This can be helpful, especially, when working with compromised system backups, where you want to be sure that your system is clean when working on a different case afterwards.

In the second part of this chapter, we demonstrated how to work with Python's **virtual environments (virtualenv)** that will be used and extended throughout the book.

In the last section of this chapter, we introduced the Python **ctypes** to you, which is a very powerful library available to the Python developer. With those **ctypes**, you are not only able to call functions in the dynamically linked libraries (available Microsoft Win32 APIs or common Linux shared objects), but they can also be used for low-level memory manipulation.

After completing this chapter, you will have a basic environment created to be used for the rest of the book, and you will also understand the fundamentals of Python **ctypes** that will be helpful in some of the following chapters.

2
Forensic Algorithms

Forensic algorithms are the building blocks for a forensic investigator. Independent from any specific implementation, these algorithms describe the details of the forensic procedures. In the first section of this chapter, we will introduce the different algorithms that are used in forensic investigations, including their advantages and disadvantages.

Algorithms

In this section, we describe the main differences between **MD5**, **SHA256**, and **SSDEEP**—the most common algorithms used in the forensic investigations. We will explain the use cases as well as the limitations and threats behind these three algorithms. This should help you understand why using SHA256 is better than using MD5 and in which cases SSDEEP can help you in the investigation.

Before we dive into the different hash functions, we will give a short summary of what a cryptographic hash function is.

A **hash function** is a function that maps an *arbitrarily large* amount of data to a value of a *fixed length*. The hash function ensures that the same input always results in the same output, called the hash sum. Consequently, a hash sum is a characteristic of a specific piece of data.

A **cryptographic hash function** is a hash function that is considered practically impossible to invert. This means that it is not possible to create the input data while having a pre-defined hash sum value by any other means than trying all the possible input values, that is *brute force*. Therefore, this class of algorithms is known as *one-way* cryptographic algorithm.

The ideal cryptographic hash function has four main properties, as follows:

1. It must be easy to compute the hash value for any given input.
2. It must be infeasible to generate the original input from its hash.
3. It must be infeasible to modify the input without changing the hash.
4. It must be infeasible to find two different inputs with the same hash (**collision-resistant**).

In the ideal case, if you create a hash of the given input and change only one bit of this input, the newly calculated hash will look totally different, as follows:

```
user@lab:~$ echo -n This is a test message | md5sum
fafb00f5732ab283681e124bf8747ed1


user@lab:~$ echo -n This is A test message | md5sum
aafb38820e0a3788eb41e9f5805e088e
```

If all of the previously mentioned properties are fulfilled, the algorithm is a cryptographically correct hash function and can be used to compare, for example, files with each other to prove that they haven't been tampered with during analysis or by an attacker.

MD5

The MD5 message-digest algorithm was the most commonly used (and is still a widely used) cryptographic hash function that produces a 128-bit (16-byte) hash value, typically expressed in the text format as a 32-digit hexadecimal number (as shown in the previous example). This message digest has been utilized in a wide variety of cryptographic applications and is commonly used to verify data integrity in forensic investigations. This algorithm was designed by Ronald Rivest in 1991 and has been heavily used since then.

A big advantage of MD5 is that it calculates faster and produces small hashes. The small hashes are a major point of interest when you need to store thousands of these hashes in a forensic investigation. Just imagine how many files a common PC will have on its hard drive. If you need to calculate a hash of each of these files and store them in a database, it would make a huge difference if each of the calculated hash has 16 byte or 32 byte of size.

Nowadays, the major disadvantage of MD5 is the fact that it is no longer considered to be collision-resistant. This means that it is possible to calculate the same hash from two different inputs. Keeping this in mind, it is not possible anymore to guarantee that a file hasn't been modified just by comparing its MD5 hash at two different stages of an investigation. At the moment it is possible to create a collision very fast, (refer to `http://www.win.tue.nl/hashclash/On%20Collisions%20for%20MD5%20-%20 M.M.J.%20Stevens.pdf`) but it is still difficult to modify a file in a way, which is now a malicious version of that benign file, and keep the MD5 hash of the original file.

The very famous cryptographer, Bruce Schneier, once wrote that (`https://www. schneier.com/blog/archives/2008/12/forging_ssl_cer.html`):

> *"We already knew that MD5 is a broken hash function" and that "no one should be using MD5 anymore".*

We would not go that far (especially because a lot of tools and services still use MD5), but you should try switching to SHA256 or at least double-check your results with the help of different hash functions in cases where it is critical. Whenever the chain of custody is crucial, we recommend using multiple hash algorithms to prove the integrity of your data.

SHA256

SHA-2 is a set of cryptographic hash functions designed by the NSA (U.S. National Security Agency) and stands for Secure Hash Algorithm 2nd Generation. It has been published in 2001 by the NIST as a U.S. federal standard (FIPS). The SHA-2 family consists of several hash functions with digests (hash values) that are between 224 bits and 512 bits. The cryptographic functions SHA256 and SHA512 are the most common versions of SHA-2 hash functions computed with 32-bit and 64-bit words.

Despite the fact that these algorithms calculate slower and that the calculated hashes are larger in size (compared to MD5), they should be the preferred algorithms that are used for integrity checks during the forensic investigations. Nowadays, SHA256 is a widely used cryptographic hash function that is still collision-resistant and entirely trustworthy.

SSDEEP

The biggest difference between **MD5**, **SHA256**, and **SSDEEP** is the fact that **SSDEEP** is not considered to be a **cryptographic hash function** as it only changes slightly when the input is changed by one bit. For example:

```
user@lab:~$ echo -n This is a test message | ssdeep
ssdeep,1.1--blocksize:hash:hash,filename
```

```
3:hMCEpFzA:hurs,"stdin"


user@lab:~$ echo -n This is A test message | ssdeep
ssdeep,1.1--blocksize:hash:hash,filename
3:hMCkrzA:hOrs,"stdin"
```

The SSDEEP packages can be downloaded and installed as described in the following URL: http://ssdeep.sourceforge.net/usage.html#install

This behavior is not a weakness of SSDEEP, it is a major advantage of this function. In reality, SSDEEP is a program to compute and match the **Context Triggered Piecewise Hashing (CTPH)** values. CTPH is a technique that is also known as **Fuzzy Hashing** and is able to match inputs that have homologies. Inputs with homologies have sequences of identical bytes in a given order with totally different bytes in between. These bytes in between can differ in content and length. CTPH, originally based on the work of *Dr. Andrew Tridgell*, was adapted by *Jesse Kornblum* and published at the DFRWS conference in 2006 in a paper called *Identifying Almost Identical Files Using Context Triggered Piecewise Hashing*; refer to http://dfrws. org/2006/proceedings/12-Kornblum.pdf.

SSDEEP can be used to check how similar the two files are and in which part of the file the difference is located. This feature is often used to check if two different applications on the mobile devices have a common code base, as shown in the following:

```
user@lab:~$ ssdeep -b malware-sample01.apk > signature.txt


user@lab:~$ cat signature.txt
Ssdeep,1.1--blocksize:hash:hash,filename
49152:FTqSf4xGvFowvJxThCwSoVpzPb03++4zlpBFrnInZWk:JqSU4ldVVpDIcz3BFr8Z7,"
malware-sample01.apk"


user@lab:~$ ssdeep -mb signature.txt malware-sample02.apk
malware-sample02.apk matches malware-sample01.apk (75)
```

In the previous example, you can see that the second sample matches the first one with a very high likelihood. These matches indicate the potential source code reuse or at least a large number of files inside the apk file are identical. A manual examination of the files in question is required to tell exactly which parts of the code or files are identical; however, we now know that both the files are similar to each other.

Supporting the chain of custody

The outcomes of forensic investigations can have a severe impact on organizations and individuals. Depending on your field of work, your investigation can become evidence in the court.

Consequently, the integrity of forensic evidence has to be ensured not just when collecting the evidence, but also throughout the entire handling and analysis. Usually, the very first step in a forensic investigation is gathering the evidence. Normally, this is done using a bitwise copy of the original media. All the subsequent analysis is performed on this forensic copy.

Creating hash sums of full disk images

To ensure that a forensic copy is actually identical to the original media, hash sums of the media and from the forensic copy are made. These hash sums must match to prove that the copy is exactly like the original data. Nowadays, it has become common to use at least two different cryptographic hash algorithms to minimize the risk of hash collisions and harden the overall process against hash collision attacks.

With Linux, one can easily create MD5 and SHA256 hashes from a drive or multiple files. In the following example, we will calculate MD5 sums and SHA256 sums for two files to provide a proof of identical content:

```
user@lab:~$ md5sum /path/to/originalfile /path/to/forensic_copy_of_sdb.
img
```

```
user@lab:~$ sha256sum /path/to/originalfile /path/to/forensic_copy_of_
sdb.img
```

This proof of identical content is required to support the chain of custody, that is, to show that the analyzed data is identical to the raw data on the disk. The term **sdb** refers to a drive attached to the forensic workstation (in Linux, the **second hard drive** is called **sdb**). To further support the chain of custody, it is highly recommended to use a write-block device between the evidence and forensic workstation to avoid any accidental change of the evidence. The second argument represents the location of a bitwise copy of the evidence. The commands output the hash sums for the original drive and the copy. The copy can be considered forensically sound if both the MD5 sums match and both the SHA256 sums match.

While the method shown in the previous example works, it has a big disadvantage, the evidence and its copy have to be read twice to calculate the hash sums. If the disk is a 1 TB hard drive, it can slow down the overall process by several hours.

The following Python code reads the data only once and feeds it into two hash calculations. Therefore, this Python script is almost twice as fast as running md5sum followed by sha256sum and produces exactly the same hash sums as these tools:

```python
#!/usr/bin/env python

import hashlib
import sys

def multi_hash(filename):
    """Calculates the md5 and sha256 hashes
       of the specified file and returns a list
       containing the hash sums as hex strings."""

    md5 = hashlib.md5()
    sha256 = hashlib.sha256()

    with open(filename, 'rb') as f:
        while True:
            buf = f.read(2**20)
            if not buf:
                break
            md5.update(buf)
            sha256.update(buf)

    return [md5.hexdigest(), sha256.hexdigest()]


if __name__ == '__main__':
    hashes = []
    print '---------- MD5 sums ----------'
    for filename in sys.argv[1:]:
        h = multi_hash(filename)
        hashes.append(h)
        print '%s  %s' % (h[0], filename)

    print '---------- SHA256 sums ----------'
    for i in range(len(hashes)):
        print '%s  %s' % (hashes[i][1], sys.argv[i+1])
```

In the following call of the script, we calculate the hash sums of some of the common Linux tools:

```
user@lab:~$ python multihash.py /bin/{bash,ls,sh}
---------- MD5 sums ----------
d79a947d06958e7826d15a5c78bfaa05   /bin/bash
fa97c59cc414e42d4e0e853ddf5b4745   /bin/ls
c01bc66da867d3e840814ec96a137aef   /bin/sh
---------- SHA256 sums ----------
cdbcb2ef76ae464ed0b22be346977355c650c5ccf61fef638308b8da60780bdd   /bin/
bash
846ac0d6c40d942300de825dbb5d517130d8a0803d22115561dcd85efee9c26b   /bin/ls
e9a7e1fd86f5aadc23c459cb05067f49cd43038f06da0c1d9f67fbcd627d622c   /bin/sh
```

It is crucial to document the hash sums of the original data and the forensic copy in the forensic report. An independent party can then read the same piece of evidence and confirm that the data that you analyzed is exactly the data of the evidence.

Creating hash sums of directory trees

Once the full image is copied, its contents should be indexed and the hash sums should be created for every file. With the support of the previously defined `multi_hash` function and Python standard libraries, a report template containing a list of all file names, sizes, and hash values can be created, as shown in the following:

```python
#!/usr/bin/env python

from datetime import datetime
import os
from os.path import join, getsize
import sys
from multihash import multi_hash

def dir_report(base_path, reportfilename):
    """Creates a report containing file integrity information.

    base_path -- The directory with the files to index
    reportfilename -- The file to write the output to"""

    with open(reportfilename, 'w') as out:
        out.write("File integrity information\n\n")
        out.write("Base path:      %s\n" % base_path)
```

```
            out.write("Report created: %s\n\n" % datetime.now().
    isoformat())
            out.write('"SHA-256","MD5","FileName","FileSize"')
            out.write("\n")

            for root, dirs, files in os.walk(base_path):
                write_dir_stats(out, root, files)

            out.write("\n\n--- END OF REPORT ---\n")

    def write_dir_stats(out, directory, files):
        """Writes status information on all specified files to the report.

        out -- open file handle of the report file
        directory -- the currently analyzed directory
        files -- list of files in that directory"""

        for name in files:
            fullname = join(directory, name)
            hashes = multi_hash(fullname)
            size = getsize(fullname)
            out.write('"%s","%s","%s",%d' % (hashes[1], hashes[0],
    fullname, size))
            out.write("\n")


    if __name__ == '__main__':
        if len(sys.argv) < 3:
            print "Usage: %s reportfile basepath\n" % sys.argv[0]
            sys.exit(1)

        dir_report(sys.argv[2], sys.argv[1])
```

This Python script is all it takes to generate the integrity information of a directory tree that includes file sizes, file names, and hash sums (SHA256, MD5). The following is an example call on our scripting directory:

```
user@lab:/home/user/dirhash $ python dirhash.py report.txt .
user@lab:/home/user/dirhash $ cat report.txt
File integrity information

Base path:      .
```

```
Report created: 2015-08-23T21:50:45.460940


"SHA-256","MD5","FileName","FileSize"

"a14f7e644d76e2e232e94fd720d35e59707a2543f01af4123abc46e8c10330cd","9c0d1
f70fffe5c59a7700b2b9bfd50cc","./multihash.py",879

"a4168e4cc7f8db611b339f4f8a949fbb57ad893f02b9a65759c793d2c8b9b4aa","bcf5a
41a403bb45974dd0ee331b1a0aa","./dirhash.py",1494

"e3b0c44298fc1c149afbf4c8996fb92427ae41e4649b934ca495991b7852b855","d41d8
cd98f00b204e9800998ecf8427e","./report.txt",0

"03047d8a202b03dfc5a310a81fd8358f37c8ba97e2fff8a0e7822cf7f36b5c83","41669
9861031e0b0d7b6d24b3de946ef","./multihash.pyc",1131



--- END OF REPORT ---
```

However, the resulting report file itself does not have any integrity protection. It is recommended to sign the resulting report, for example, using **GnuPG**, as shown in the following:

```
user@lab:~$ gpg --clearsign report.txt
```

If you have never used gpg before, you need to generate a private key before you can sign the documents. This can be done with the gpg --gen-key command. Consult https://www.gnupg.org/documentation for more details about GnuPG and its use. This creates an additional report.txt.asc file containing the original report and a digital signature. Any subsequent modification of that file invalidates the digital signature.

> The techniques described here are merely the examples of how to support the chain of custody. If the forensic analysis is to be used in the court, it is highly recommended to seek legal advice about the chain-of-custody requirements in your legislation.

Real-world scenarios

This section will demonstrate some use cases where the preceding algorithms and techniques are used to support the investigator. For this chapter, we use two very common and interesting examples, **Mobile Malware** and the **National Software Reference Library (NSRL)**.

Mobile Malware

In this example, we will check the installed applications on an Android smartphone against an online analysis system, **Mobile-Sandbox**. Mobile-Sandbox is a website that provides free Android files checking for viruses or suspicious behavior, `http://www.mobilesandbox.org`. It is connected to **VirusTotal**, which uses up to 56 different antivirus products and scan engines to check for viruses that the user's antivirus solution may have missed or verify against any false positives. Additionally, Mobile-Sandbox uses custom techniques to detect applications that act potentially malicious. Antivirus software vendors, developers, and researchers behind Mobile-Sandbox can receive copies of the files to help in improving their software and techniques.

In the example, we will use two steps to successfully compare the installed applications with the already tested apps on the Mobile-Sandbox web service.

The first step is to get the hash sums of the installed applications on the device. This is very important as these values can help to identify the apps and check them against the online services. For this example, we will use an application from Google Play, **AppExtract** (https://play.google.com/store/apps/details?id=de.mspreitz. appextract). The forensically more correct way of getting these values can be found in *Chapter 6, Using Python for Mobile Forensics*.

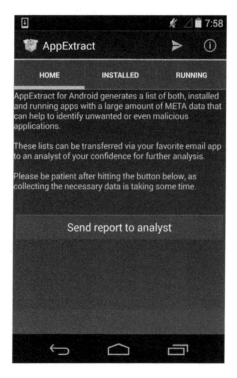

AppExtract for Android generates a list of installed and running apps with a large amount of metadata that can help in identifying unwanted or even malicious applications. This metadata contains the SHA256 hash sum of the application packages, an indicator whether the app has been installed by the user or the system itself, and a lot of additional data that can help in identifying if the app is benign or not. These lists can be transferred via your favorite email app for further analysis. Once you receive the plain-text email with the generated lists, you just need to copy the list that contains all the installed applications to a CSV file. This file can be used for an automated analysis or opened with **LibreOffice Calc** in the lab environment. You can see the metadata of the current version of the Chrome Browser for Android in the following:

```
Type;App_Name;md5;TargetSdkVersion;Package_Name;Process_Name;APK_
Location;Version_Code;Version_Name;Certificate_Info;Certificate_
SN;InstallTime;LastModified


SystemApp;Chrome;4e4c56a8a7d8d6b1ec3e0149b3918656;21;com.android.
chrome;com.android.chrome;/data/app/com.android.chrome-2.apk;2311109;
42.0.2311.109;CN=Android, OU=Android, O=Google Inc., L=Mountain View,
ST=California, C=US;14042372374541250701;unknown;unknown
```

The second step is to compare the hash sums from the device (third column in our CSV file) with the Mobile-Sandbox database. This can be done with the help of the following script that we will save as get_infos_mobilesandbox.py:

```python
#!/usr/bin/env python

import sys, requests

# Authentication Parameters
# if you need an API key and user name please contact @m_spreitz
API_FORMAT = 'json'
API_USER = ''
API_KEY = ''

# parsing input parameters
if (len(sys.argv) < 3):
    print "Get infos to a specific Android app from the Mobile-
Sandbox."
    print "Usage: %s requests [type (md5,sha256)] [value]" % sys.
argv[0]
    sys.exit(0)

# building the payload
payload = {'format':API_FORMAT,
```

```
                    'username':API_USER,
                    'api_key':API_KEY,
                    'searchType':str(sys.argv[1]),    # has to be md5 or sha256
                    'searchValue':str(sys.argv[2])}

    # submitting sample hash and getting meta data
    print "-------------------------------"
    r = requests.get("http://mobilesandbox.org/api/bot/queue/get_info/",
    params=payload)

    # printing result and writing report file to disk
    if not r.status_code == requests.codes.ok:
        print "query result: \033[91m" + r.text + "\033[0m"
    else:
        for key, value in r.json().iteritems():
            print key + ": \033[94m" + str(value) + "\033[0m"
    print "-------------------------------"
```

The script can be used as shown in the following:

```
(labenv)user@lab:~$ ./get_infos_mobilesandbox.py md5
4e4c56a8a7d8d6b1ec3e0149b3918656


-------------------------------
status: done
min_sdk_version: 0
package_name: com.android.chrome
apk_name: Chrome.apk
AV_detection_rate: 0 / 56
drebin_score: benign (1.38173)
sample_origin: user upload
android_build_version: Android 1.0
ssdeep: 196608:ddkkKqfC+ca8eE/jXQewwn5ux1aDn9PpvPBic6aQmAHQXPOo:dBKZaJYXQ
E5u3ajtpvpeaQm1
sha256: 79de1dc6af66e6830960d6f991cc3e416fd3ce63fb786db6954a3ccaa7f7323c
malware_family: ---
md5: 4e4c56a8a7d8d6b1ec3e0149b3918656
-------------------------------
```

With the help of these three tools, it is possible to quickly check if an application on a mobile device is potentially infected (see the highlighted parts in the response) or at least where to start with the manual investigation if an application hasn't been tested before.

NSRLquery

To increase efficiency in the forensic analysis, it is crucial to sort out any files that belong to known software and have not been modified. The **National Software Reference Library** (**NSRL**) maintains multiple lists of hash sums for the known content. NSRL is a project of the U.S. Department of Homeland Security, further details are available on http://www.nsrl.nist.gov/. It is important to understand that these lists of hash sums merely indicate that a file was not modified as compared to the version that was submitted to the NSRL. Consequently, it is normal that a lot of files, which are to be analysed during a forensic investigation, are not listed in NSRL. On the other hand, even the listed files can be used and deployed by an attacker as a tool. For example, a tool such as psexec.exe is a program provided by Microsoft for remote administration and listed in NSRL. Nevertheless, an attacker may have deployed it for his malicious purposes.

Which NSRL list should be used?

NSRL consists of several hash sets. It is highly recommended to begin with the *minimal set*. This set only contains one hash sum per file, which means only one file version is known.

The minimal set is offered free of charge to download on the NIST homepage. The download consists of a single ZIP file with the hash list and a list of supported software products as the most prominent contents.

The hashes are stored in the NSRLFile.txt file that holds one file hash per line, for example:

```
"3CACD2048DB88F4F2E863B6DE3B1FD197922B3F2","0BEA3F79A36B1F67B2CE0F5955
24C77C","C39B9F35","TWAIN.DLL",94784,14965,"358",""
```

The fields of this record are as follows:

- The hash sum of the file that is calculated with SHA-1, a predecessor to the SHA-256 algorithm described earlier.

- The hash sum of the file that is calculated with MD5.

- The CRC32 checksum of the file.

- The file name.

- The file size in bytes.

- A product code denoting the software product this file belongs to. The `NSRLProd.txt` file contains a list of all products and can be used to look up the product code. In the previous example, the code `14965` denotes Microsoft Picture It!.

- The operating system where this file is to be expected. The list of operating system codes can be found in `NSRLOS.txt`.

- An indicator whether this file is to be considered normal (""), a malicious file ("N"), or special ("S"). While this flag is part of the specification, all the files of the current NSRL minimal set are set to be normal.

More details about the file specifications can be found at `http://www.nsrl.nist.gov/Documents/Data-Formats-of-the-NSRL-Reference-Data-Set-16.pdf`.

Downloading and installing nsrlsvr

Currently, the NSRL database contains more than 40 million distinct hashes in the minimal set. A text-based search would take minutes, even on an up-to-date workstation. Therefore, it is important to make efficient lookups to that database. Rob Hanson's tool **nsrlsvr** provides a server that supports efficient lookups. It is available at `https://rjhansen.github.io/nsrlsvr/`.

There are also public NSRL servers on the Internet that you can use. These are usually provided on an *as is* basis. However, to test smaller sets of hashes, you may use Robert Hanson's public server `nsrllookup.com` and continue reading with the next section.

To compile the software on a Linux system, the automake, autoconf, and c++ compiler tools must be installed. The detailed installation instructions including all the requirements are provided in the `INSTALL` file.

Installing nsrlsvr in a non-default directory

The installation directory of nsrlsvr can be changed by calling the `configure` script with the `--prefix` parameter. The parameter value denotes the target directory. If a user-writable directory is specified, the installation does not require root privileges and can be completely removed by removing the installation directory.

The nsrlsrv maintains its own copy of all the MD5 hash sums of the NSRL database. Therefore, it is required to initialize the hash database. The required nsrlupdate tool is provided with nsrlsrv.

```
user@lab:~$ nsrlupdate your/path/to/NSRLFile.txt
```

After the database is fully populated, the server can be started by simply calling:

```
user@lab:~$ nsrlsvr
```

If everything is installed correctly, this command returns without providing any output and the server starts listening to the TCP port 9120 for requests.

Writing a client for nsrlsvr in Python

There is also a client tool for using nsrlsvr called **nsrllookup**. The client is written in C++ and available at `https://rjhansen.github.io/nsrllookup/`. However, a client for interacting with nsrlsvr can easily be implemented in native Python. This section explains the protocol and shows a sample implementation of such a client.

The nsrlsvr implements a text-oriented protocol on its network port 9120. Every command consists of one line of text followed by a newline (CR LF). The following commands are supported:

- **version: 2.0**: The version command is used for the initial handshake between the nsrl client and nsrlsvr. The client is supposed to provide its version after the colon. The server will always respond with OK followed by a line break.

- **query 5CB360EF546633691912089DB24A82EE 908A54EB629F410C647A573F91E80775 BFDD76C4DD6F8C0C2474215AD5E193CF**: The query command is used for actually querying the NSRL database from the server. The keyword **query** is followed by one or multiple MD5 hash sums. The server will respond with OK followed by a sequence of zeroes and ones. A 1 indicates that the MD5 hash sum was found in the database and a 0 indicates that there was no match. For example, the query shown previously would lead to the following answer:

  ```
  OK 101
  ```

  This means that the first and the last MD5 hashes were found in NSRL, but the middle hash sum could not be found.

- **BYE**: The bye command terminates the connection to the nsrlsvr.

Consequently, the following Python routine is sufficient to efficiently query the NSRL database:

```python
#!/usr/bin/env python

import socket

NSRL_SERVER='127.0.0.1'
NSRL_PORT=9120

def nsrlquery(md5hashes):
    """Query the NSRL server and return a list of booleans.

    Arguments:
    md5hashes -- The list of MD5 hashes for the query.
    """

    s = socket.socket(socket.AF_INET, socket.SOCK_STREAM)
    s.connect((NSRL_SERVER, NSRL_PORT))

    try:
        f = s.makefile('r')
        s.sendall("version: 2.0\r\n")
        response = f.readline();
        if response.strip() != 'OK':
            raise RuntimeError('NSRL handshake error')

        query = 'query ' + ' '.join(md5hashes) + "\r\n"
        s.sendall(query)
        response = f.readline();

        if response[:2] != 'OK':
            raise RuntimeError('NSRL query error')

        return [c=='1' for c in response[3:].strip()]
    finally:
        s.close()
```

Using this module is as easy as shown here:

```python
import nsrlquery
hashes = ['86d3d86902b09d963afc08ea0002a746',
          '3dcfe9688ca733a76f82d03d7ef4a21f',
          '976fe1fe512945e390ba10f6964565bf']
nsrlquery.nsrlquery(hashes)
```

This code queries the NSRL server and returns a list of booleans, each indicating whether the corresponding MD5 hash has been found in the NSRL file list.

Summary

This chapter provided an overview of the domains of the forensic and example algorithms for each of these domains. We also showed you how to compare applications installed on an Android device with web services such as **Mobile-Sandbox**. In the second real-world example, we demonstrated how to sort out benign and known files from a Windows system to reduce the amount of data that is to be analyzed manually. With **NSRLquery**, the forensic investigations can focus on new or modified content and do not need to waste time on the widely known content of standard applications.

In the following chapters, these algorithms will be applied to a selection of device types, operating systems, and applications for use during forensic investigation.

3

Using Python for Windows and Linux Forensics

In this chapter, we will focus on the parts of the forensic investigation that are specific to the operating systems. We chose the most widely used operating systems on the desktop and server systems—Microsoft Windows and Linux.

For both operating systems, we selected examples of interesting evidence and how to automate its analysis using Python. Consequently, in this chapter, you will learn the following:

- Analyzing the foundations of the Windows event log, selecting interesting parts, and automatically parsing them

- Organizing the Windows Registry and efficiently searching for **Indicators of Compromise (IOC)**

- Searching Linux local account information for IOC

- Understanding, using, and parsing Linux file metadata with POSIX ACL and file based capabilities as the most prominent extensions to the standard metadata

Analyzing the Windows Event Log

Windows includes many monitoring and logging capabilities and traces data and events for a large amount and variety of activities occurring in the operating system. The vast number of events, which can be logged, does neither make it easy for an administrator to identify the specific important events nor helps a forensic investigator to find Indicators of Compromise. Therefore, we will start this section with a small introduction to the Windows Event Log and the changes in its format over time, followed by a description of the important event types that should help an investigator to quickly find suspicious actions in the large amount of other events. In the last section of this chapter, we will demonstrate how to parse the Event Log and automatically find the potential IOCs (e.g., user logons, service creation, and so on).

The Windows Event Log

According to Microsoft, Windows Event Log files are special files that record significant events, such as when a user logs on to the computer or when a program encounters an error, (refer to `http://windows.microsoft.com/en-us/windows/what-information-event-logs-event-viewer#1TC=windows-7`). Whenever these types of events occur, Windows records the event in an event log that can be read using Event Viewer or similar tools.

With the release of Windows 7 and Windows Server 2008, Microsoft has performed a major change in their Event Log technique. They changed from the classical **Windows Event Log (EVT)** to the newer **Windows XML Event Log (EVTX)**. In the following paragraphs, we will explain some of the main differences between these two log file types.

Due to the fact that Microsoft no longer supports Windows XP and Server 2003 is in the extended support stage at present (meaning that it will go out of support very soon), there are XP and 2003 systems still out there. Thus, some investigators are still going to need to know the difference between the older EVT and the new EVTX and the possible problems arising during analysis of these files.

Besides the binary differences in the records and the Event Log files themselves, the amount of these log files differs too. On a Windows XP/2003 system, there were three main Event Log files: **System**, **Application**, and **Security**. They are stored in the `C:\Windows\system32\config` directory. The server versions of the OS may maintain additional Event Logs (DNS Server, Directory Service, File Replication Service, and so on) depending upon the functionality of the server. On a current Windows 7 system, you can find more than 143 files full of event logs. This gets even more if you compare it to the newer server versions of Microsoft Windows.

The EVT log records only contain a very small amount of human-readable content and are made human readable through tools such as the event viewer at analysis time. These tools combine the predefined log templates that are commonly stored in the system's DLL or EXE files with the data stored in the EVT file itself. When one of the various log viewing tools displays log records, it has to determine which DLL files will store the message templates. This meta-information is stored in the Windows Registry and is specific to each type of the previously mentioned three main Event Log files (System, Application, and Security).

All of the earlier mentioned details follow the fact that the EVT files aren't really useful without their corresponding metafiles, which store the core meaning of the log. This creates two major analysis problems:

- First, an attacker could modify DLL files or the Windows Registry in order to change the meaning of event logs without having to touch the EVT file.

- Second, when the software is uninstalled on a system, it could result in the EVT records losing their context.

As an investigator, one must carefully keep these issues in mind when analyzing EVT logs and also when writing those logs to remote systems for later analysis. An even more detailed analysis of the EVT records can be found in the ForensicsWiki, `http://forensicswiki.org/wiki/Windows_Event_Log_(EVT)`.

In comparison to EVT, the EVTX files are stored as a binary XML file format. On the newer Windows systems, the event logs can be viewed and analyzed with either the Event Viewer or a vast number of other programs and tools (in the following sections, we will describe some Python scripts that can be used too). When using the Event Viewer, one has to bear in mind that this program can represent the EVTX files in two different formats: **general** and **detailed**. The general (sometimes called formatted) view can hide significant event data that is stored in the event record and can only be seen in the detailed view. Thus, if you are planning to use the Event Viewer for analyzing the EVTX files, always use the detailed option to display the files.

If you are interested in a more detailed analysis of the EVTX file format, you should take a look at the ForensicsWiki, `http://forensicswiki.org/wiki/Windows_XML_Event_Log_(EVTX)`. Another great explanation of the deeper EVTX file format details has been presented by *Andreas Schuster* at DFRWS 2007, refer to `http://www.dfrws.org/2007/proceedings/p65-schuster_pres.pdf`. This presentation can be very helpful if you want to understand the details of the binary XML format or write your own parsers of EVTX files.

If you need to open the EVT files on a Windows 7 or newer system, it's best to convert the older EVT file to the EVTX syntax before opening it. This can be done in several ways as described in a technet.com blog post, `http://blogs.technet.com/b/askperf/archive/2007/10/12/windows-vista-and-exported-event-log-files.aspx`.

Interesting Events

A full list of Windows events on the newer system can be found in a knowledge base article of Microsoft at, `https://support.microsoft.com/en-us/kb/947226`. As the number of these events is getting bigger with every new version of the system and every newly installed application, you can easily find more than several hundreds of different event types on a single Windows system. Due to this fact, we tried to sort out some interesting event types that can be helpful when analyzing a system or reconstructing user events (a more detailed explanation of which Event Logs can be helpful under what conditions can also be found in TSA-13-1004-SG, `https://www.nsa.gov/ia/_files/app/spotting_the_adversary_with_windows_event_log_monitoring.pdf`):

- **EMET (1, 2)**: If the organization is actively using the Microsoft **Enhanced Mitigation Experience Toolkit (EMET)**, then these logs can be very helpful during investigation.

- **Windows-Update-Failure (20, 24, 25, 31, 34, 35)**: The failure to update issues should be addressed to avoid prolonging the existence of an application issue or vulnerability in the operating system or an application. Sometimes, this also helps in identifying infections of a system.

- **Microsoft-Windows-Eventlog (104, 1102)**: It is unlikely that event log data would be cleared during normal operations and it is more likely that a malicious attacker may try to cover their tracks by clearing an event log. When an event log gets cleared, it is suspicious.

- **Microsoft-Windows-TaskScheduler (106)**: It displays newly registered Scheduled Tasks. This can be very helpful if you are searching for signs of malware infections.

- **McAfee-Log-Event (257)**: McAfee malware detection — McAfee AntiVirus may detect malware behaviors without actually detecting the EXE file itself. This can be very valuable in determining how the malware got into a system. In general, the event logs of the installed AV solution are very valuable logs when starting an analysis of a potentially compromised system. Therefore, you should remind yourself where to find those logs in the Event Log.

- **Microsoft-Windows-DNS-Client (1014)**: DNS name resolution timeout; this event type can also be very helpful when searching for malware or when trying to find out whether a user has tried to connect to a specific website or service.

- **Firewall-Rule-Add/Change/Delete (2004, 2005, 2006, 2033)**: If the client workstations are taking advantage of the built-in host-based Windows Firewall, then there is value in collecting events to track the firewall status. Normal users should not be modifying the firewall rules of their local machine.

- **Microsoft-Windows-Windows Defender (3004)**: Windows Defender malware detection logs.

- **Microsoft-Windows-Security-Auditing (4720, 4724, 4725, 4728, 4732, 4635, 4740, 4748, 4756)**: In these logs, you can find information such as remote desktop logins and users that have been added to privileged groups, and account lockouts can also be tracked. User accounts that are being promoted to the privileged groups should be audited very closely to ensure that the users are, in fact, supposed to be in a privileged group. Unauthorized membership of the privileged groups is a strong indicator that a malicious activity has occurred.

- **Service-Control-Manager (7030, 7045)**: It monitors whether a service is configured to interact with the desktop or has been installed on the system in general.

- **App-Locker-Block/Warning (8003, 8004, 8006, 8007)**: Application whitelisting events should be collected to look for the applications that have been blocked from execution. Any blocked application could be malware or the users trying to run an unapproved software.

Harlan Carvey stated in one of his blog posts (`http://windowsir.blogspot.de/2014/10/windows-event-logs.html`) that beyond individual event records (source/ID pairs), one of the aspects of the newer versions of Windows (in particular, Windows 7) is that there are a lot of events that are being recorded by default across multiple Event Log files. Thus, when some events occur, multiple event records are stored in different Event Log types and often across different Event Log files. For example, when a user logs in to a system on the console, there will be an event recorded in the security event log, a couple of events will be recorded in the `Microsoft-Windows-TerminalServices-LocalSessionManager/Operational` log, and a couple of events will also be recorded in the `Microsoft-Windows-TaskScheduler/Operational` log.

The Event Log can also be used to detect whether an attacker has used some kind of anti-forensic techniques. One of those techniques would be to change the system time in order to mislead an investigator. To detect this kind of modification, an investigator has to list all the available Event Log records by the sequence number and generated time. If the system time has been rolled back, there would be a point where the time an event has been generated was before the previous event. Some more examples of detecting anti-forensic techniques with the help of Windows Event Log can be found in a blog post by *Harlan Carvey*, at `http://windowsir.blogspot.de/2013/07/howto-determinedetect-use-of-anti.html`.

Parsing the Event Log for IOC

When talking about Event Logs and analyzing these logs with Python, there is no way to get around **python-evtx**. These scripts (`https://github.com/williballenthin/python-evtx`) have been developed using the 2.7+ tags of the Python programming language. As it is purely Python, the module works equally well across the platforms. The code does not depend on any modules that require separate compilation and operates on the event log files from the Windows operating systems that are newer than Windows Vista that is EVTX.

The second tool that we want to bring to your attention is **plaso**, (refer to `http://plaso.kiddaland.net/`). This tool set has evolved from **log2timeline** and is now build in Python. With the help of this tool set, you can create meaningful timelines of the system events and other log files (for example, Apache). There is also a very good cheat sheet, `http://digital-forensics.sans.org/media/log2timeline_cheatsheet.pdf`, for log2timeline that demonstrates the real power of this tool. One of the big advantages of this tool set is the fact that you can even run it on a full image of a system to generate a timeline of all actions that the users performed on that system before creating the image.

In the following sections, we will show some examples of how to use python-evtx to find IOC in the Windows Event Log and how plaso will help you identify more IOCs and display them in a nicely formatted timeline.

The python-evtx parser

First of all, we want to start with a basic conversion of the binary XML format of EVTX files to the readable XML files. This can be done using `evtxdump.py`, `https://github.com/williballenthin/python-evtx`, which will also be the basis of our following scripts:

```
#!/usr/bin/env python
import mmap
import contextlib
```

```
import argparse

from Evtx.Evtx import FileHeader
from Evtx.Views import evtx_file_xml_view

def main():
    parser = argparse.ArgumentParser(description="Dump a binary EVTX
file into XML.")
    parser.add_argument("--cleanup", action="store_true",
help="Cleanup unused XML entities (slower)"),
    parser.add_argument("evtx", type=str, help="Path to the Windows
EVTX event log file")
    args = parser.parse_args()

    with open(args.evtx, 'r') as f:
        with contextlib.closing(mmap.mmap(f.fileno(), 0, access=mmap.
ACCESS_READ)) as buf:

            fh = FileHeader(buf, 0x0)
            print "<?xml version=\"1.0\" encoding=\"utf-8\"
standalone=\"yes\" ?>"
            print "<Events>"
            for xml, record in evtx_file_xml_view(fh):
                print xml
            print "</Events>"

if __name__ == "__main__":
    main()
```

When dumping a logon event (event id 4724) with the help of the previously mentioned script, the result will look similar to the following:

```
<Event xmlns="http://schemas.microsoft.com/win/2004/08/events/
event"><System><Provider Name="Microsoft-Windows-Security-Auditing"
Guid="54849625-5478-4994-a5ba-3e3b0328c30d"></Provider>
<EventID Qualifiers="">4724</EventID>
<Version>0</Version>
<Level>0</Level>
<Task>13824</Task>
<Opcode>0</Opcode>
<Keywords>0x8020000000000000</Keywords>
<TimeCreated SystemTime="2013-11-21 10:40:51.552799"></TimeCreated>
<EventRecordID>115</EventRecordID>
<Correlation ActivityID="" RelatedActivityID=""></Correlation>
<Execution ProcessID="452" ThreadID="1776"></Execution>
<Channel>Security</Channel>
```

```
<Computer>windows</Computer>
<Security UserID=""></Security>
</System>
<EventData><Data Name="TargetUserName">mspreitz</Data>
<Data Name="TargetDomainName">windows</Data>
<Data Name="TargetSid"
>S-1-5-21-3147386740-1191307685-1965871575-1000</Data>
<Data Name="SubjectUserSid">S-1-5-18</Data>
<Data Name="SubjectUserName">WIN-PC9VCSAQB0H$</Data>
<Data Name="SubjectDomainName">WORKGROUP</Data>
<Data Name="SubjectLogonId">0x00000000000003e7</Data>
</EventData>
</Event>
```

When using evtxdump.py, https://github.com/williballenthin/python-evtx, with a large Windows Event Log file, the output will be very large as you will find all the recorded logs in the generated XML file. For an analyst, it is often important to perform a fast triage or search for specific events quickly. Due to this, we modify the script in a way that it is possible to extract only specific events, as shown in the following:

```python
#!/usr/bin/env python
import mmap
import contextlib
import argparse
from xml.dom import minidom

from Evtx.Evtx import FileHeader
from Evtx.Views import evtx_file_xml_view

def main():
    parser = argparse.ArgumentParser(description="Dump specific event
ids from a binary EVTX file into XML.")
    parser.add_argument("--cleanup", action="store_true",
help="Cleanup unused XML entities (slower)"),
    parser.add_argument("evtx", type=str, help="Path to the Windows
EVTX event log file")
    parser.add_argument("out", type=str, help="Path and name of the
output file")
    parser.add_argument("--eventID", type=int, help="Event id that
should be extracted")
    args = parser.parse_args()

    outFile = open(args.out, 'a+')
    with open(args.evtx, 'r') as f:
```

```
        with contextlib.closing(mmap.mmap(f.fileno(), 0, access=mmap.
ACCESS_READ)) as buf:
            fh = FileHeader(buf, 0x0)
            outFile.write("<?xml version=\"1.0\" encoding=\"utf-8\"
standalone=\"yes\" ?>")
            outFile.write("<Events>")
            for xml, record in evtx_file_xml_view(fh):
                xmldoc = minidom.parseString(xml)
                event_id = xmldoc.getElementsByTagName('EventID')[0].
childNodes[0].nodeValue
                if event_id == str(args.eventID):
                    outFile.write(xml)
                else:
                    continue
            outFile.write("</Events>")

if __name__ == "__main__":
    main()
```

If you now want to extract all logon events from the security event log of a Windows system in a given XML file, you just have to execute the script as follows:

```
user@lab:~$ ./evtxdump.py security.evtx logon_events.xml -eventID 4724
```

The plaso and log2timeline tools

In this section, we will demonstrate how to find logon and logoff events on a Terminal Server. The Terminal Services logon and logoff events can be tagged using `plasm` and filtered using `psort` to get a quick overview of which users have been logging in to a machine and when and where from. This information can be very helpful when searching for compromises. To start with plaso, you first need to tag all your data. Tagging with plaso is as easy as shown in the following:

```
user@lab:~$ ./plasm.py tag --tagfile=tag_windows.txt storage_file
```

After successful tagging, you can search the storage file for tags with the following command:

```
user@lab:~$ ./psort.py storage_file "tag contains 'Session logon
succeeded'"
```

The result of this command execution will show you all the successful logon events on a given system. Similar commands can be executed when searching for the services that are started or EMET failures.

Now, that you have seen the kind of data that you are able to extract from Windows Event Log, we will show you a second component of Microsoft Windows that is really helpful when searching for IOC or when trying to reconstruct the user behavior.

Analyzing the Windows Registry

The Windows Registry is one of the essential components of the current Microsoft Windows operating systems and thus also a very important point in a forensic investigation. It performs two critical tasks for the Windows operating system. First, it is the repository of settings for the Windows operating system and the applications that are installed on the system. Second, it is the database of the configuration of all installed hardware. Microsoft defines the registry as follows:

> *"A central hierarchical database used in Microsoft Windows 98, Windows CE, Windows NT, and Windows 2000 used to store information that is necessary to configure the system for one or more users, applications and hardware devices."*
> *(Microsoft Computer Dictionary)*

In the following sections, we will explain several elements of the Windows Registry that may be important to a forensics investigator and that help in understanding where to find the most valuable indicators. We will start with an overview of the structure to help you find your way through the large amount of data in the registry. Afterwards, we will demonstrate some helpful scripts to extract indicators of compromise (IOC).

Windows Registry Structure

In the Windows operating system, the Windows Registry is organized logically in a number of root keys. There are five logical root keys in the Windows Registry of a Windows 7 system, as shown in the following:

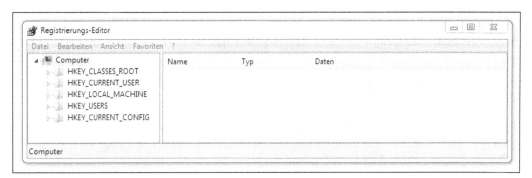

The previous figure shows the five root keys of the Registry in a Windows 7 system that are displayed by the Windows Registry Editor (one of the most common tools to view and examine the Windows Registry).

There are two kinds of root keys: volatile and nonvolatile. There are only two root keys that are stored on the hard disk of the system and are nonvolatile data held in the main memory: **HKEY_LOCAL_MACHINE** and **HKEY_USERS**. The other root keys are either the subsets of these keys or are the volatile keys that can only be examined during the runtime or when dumping the memory of a system before starting the analysis of its image.

The Windows operating system organizes the Registry in a number of hive files. According to Microsoft, (refer to `https://msdn.microsoft.com/en-us/library/windows/desktop/ms724877%28v=vs.85%29.aspx`), the hive is defined as follows:

> *A hive is a logical group of keys, sub keys, and values in the registry that has a set of supporting files containing backups of its data.*

If a new user logs on a Windows machine, a User Profile Hive is created. This hive contains specific registry information (for example, application settings, desktop environment, network connections, and printers) and is located in the **HKEY_USERS** key.

Each hive has additional supporting files that are stored in the `%SystemRoot%\System32\Config` directory. These files are updated each time a user logs on and the filename extensions of the files in these directories indicate the type of data that they contain. Refer to the following table for more details (reference taken from `https://msdn.microsoft.com/en-us/library/windows/desktop/ms724877%28v=vs.85%29.aspx`):

Extension	Description
none	A complete copy of the hive data.
.alt	A backup copy of the critical HKEY_LOCAL_MACHINE\System hive. Only the System key has an .alt file.
.log	A transaction log of changes to the keys and value entries in the hive.
.sav	A backup copy of a hive.

In the following section, we will discuss where to find interesting hives and how to analyze them with the help of the Python tools.

Parsing the Registry for IOC

In this section, we will discuss which registry hives are important when searching for IOC. These subsections include the following topics:

- **Connected USB Devices**: This section will show which devices had been connected to a system and when. This helps in identifying the possible ways of data leakage or exfiltration through a system user.

- **User Histories**: This section will show where to find histories of the opened files.

- **Startup Programs**: This section will show which programs will be executed on system start. This can be very helpful when trying to identify the infected systems.

- **System Information**: This section will show where to find important information of the system in question (for example, usernames).

- **Shim Cache Parser**: This section will show how to get important IOC with the help of common Python tools such as Mandiant's **Shim Cache Parser**, refer to `https://www.mandiant.com/blog/leveraging-application-compatibility-cache-forensic-investigations/`.

Connected USB Devices

One of the most common questions that an incident response person has to answer is whether a user has exfiltrated confidential data from a system or whether a system compromise has been initiated by a rogue USB device that a user connected to the system. To answer this question, the Windows Registry is a good point to start.

Any time a new USB device is connected to the system, it will leave information in the registry. This information can uniquely identify each USB device that has been connected to the system. The registry stores the vendor ID, product ID, revision and serial numbers of each connected USB device. This information can be found in the `HKEY_LOCAL_MACHINE\SYSTEM\ControlSet001\Enum\USBSTOR` registry hive, *Windows Forensic Analysis*, *Harlan Carvey*, *Dave Kleiman*, *Syngress Publishing*, which is also shown in the following screenshot:

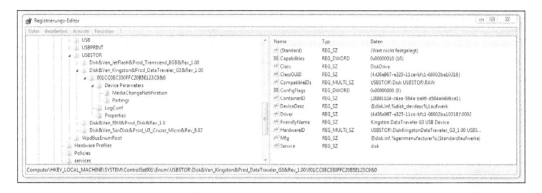

User histories

On a Windows system, there are several lists in the Registry that help in identifying the recent user activity (for example, recently visited web pages or recently opened Microsoft Word files). The following table shows some of these lists with the corresponding Windows Registry subkeys, for all lists and their Windows Registry subkeys refer to `http://ro.ecu.edu.au/cgi/viewcontent.cgi?article=1071&context=adf`:

History list	Related windows registry sub key
Typed URLs in Microsoft Internet Explorer	HKEY_USERS\S-1-5-21-[User Identifier] \Software\ Microsoft\Internet Explorer\TypedURLs
Most recently used Microsoft Office files	HKEY_USERS\S-1-5-21-[User Identifier] \Software \ Microsoft\Office\12.0\Office_App_Name\File MRU
Most recently mapped network drives	HKEY_USERS\S-1-5-21-[User Identifier] \Software \ Microsoft\Windows\CurrentVersion\Explorer\Map Network Drive MRU
Most recently typed command on the RUN dialog	HKEY_USERS\S-1-5-21-[User Identifier] \Software \ Microsoft\Windows\CurrentVersion\Explorer\RunMRU
Recent folders	HKEY_USERS\S-1-5-21-[User Identifier] \Software\ Microsoft\Windows\CurrentVersion\Explorer\RecentDocs\ Folder

Startup programs

During some investigations, it is important to find out which software was automatically run at startup and which software was manually started by a user. To help answer this question, the Windows Registry HKEY_LOCAL_MACHINE\SOFTWARE\ Microsoft\Windows\CurrentVersion\Run can help again. The list of startup programs is shown in the following figure and is listed within the *Windows Register hive*, which is taken from *A Windows Registry Quick Reference, Farmer, D. J*:

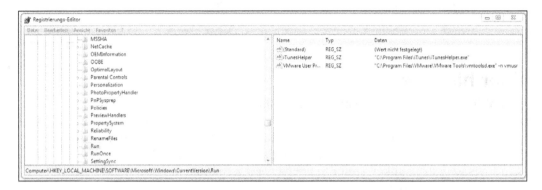

System Information

In this section, we will see some registry hives that can be important when analyzing a system. First of all, there is a large amount of information about the user account that is stored in the registry, as follows:

- A list of user accounts
- Last login time of each account
- Whether the account requires a password
- Whether a specific account is disabled or enabled
- The hash technique that is used for calculating the password hash

All of this information is held in the following registry key:

HKEY_LOCAL_MACHINE\SAM\Domains\Account\Users

There is a lot more interesting data in the Windows Registry; however, one type of information can be very helpful during a forensic investigation: the time of the last shutdown of the system. This information is stored in the ShutdownTime value in the following hive:

HKEY_LOCAL_MACHINE\SYSTEM\ControlSet001\Control\Windows

This information is often interesting on server systems as it could be a hint as to when the last updates had been applied or whether there had been any unplanned reboots of a system, which also could have been caused by an attacker.

Shim Cache Parser

The Windows Registry contains application compatibility issues and a large amount of metadata (such as file size, file's last modified time, and last execution time depending on the operating system version) that could be important for the application runtime in **Application Compatibility Shim Cache**.

 The implementation and structure of the Application Compatibility Shim Cache can vary per operating system. Thus, check your findings thoroughly.

Data about application compatibility and runtime issues can be very useful during an incident response or any other kind of forensic investigation in order to identify the potentially infected systems and to create a timeline of when the potential infection took place. Mandiant has released a tool to extract this kind of evidence: **Shim Cache Parser,** (for more information refer to `https://github.com/mandiant/ShimCacheParser`)

> *Shim Cache Parser will automatically determine the format of the cached data and output their contents. It supports a number of inputs including system registry hives, raw binary, or the current system's registry.*

The tool can be used against an exported registry hive or against the running system. When using it against a running system, you just need to execute the following command:

```
C:\tools\mandiant> python ShimCacheParser.py -l -o out.csv


[+] Dumping Shim Cache data from the current system...
[+] Found 64bit Windows 7/2k8-R2 Shim Cache data...
[+] Found 64bit Windows 7/2k8-R2 Shim Cache data...
[+] Found 64bit Windows 7/2k8-R2 Shim Cache data...
[+] Writing output to out.csv...
```

When looking at the generated CSV output, you can find installed applications and first runtime of these files, as follows:

```
Last Modified,Last Update,Path,File Size,Exec Flag

05/04/11 05:19:28,N/A,C:\Windows\system32\SearchFilterHost.exe,N/A,True

05/24/15 16:44:45,N/A,C:\Program Files (x86)\Avira\AntiVir Desktop\avwsc.
exe,N/A,True

11/21/10 03:24:15,N/A,C:\Windows\system32\wbem\wmiprvse.exe,N/A,True

05/30/14 08:07:49,N/A,C:\Windows\TEMP\40F00A21-D2E7-47A3-AE16-
0AFB8E6C1F87\dismhost.exe,N/A,True

07/14/09 01:39:02,N/A,C:\Windows\system32\DeviceDisplayObjectProvider.
exe,N/A,True

07/26/13 02:24:56,N/A,C:\Windows\System32\shdocvw.dll,N/A,False

05/24/15 16:46:22,N/A,C:\Program Files (x86)\Google\Update\1.3.27.5\
GoogleCrashHandler.exe,N/A,True

05/07/15 21:42:59,N/A,C:\Windows\system32\GWX\GWX.exe,N/A,True

03/26/15 20:57:08,N/A,C:\Program Files (x86)\Parallels\Parallels Tools\
prl_cc.exe,N/A,True

10/07/14 16:29:54,N/A,C:\Program Files (x86)\KeePass Password Safe 2\
KeePass.exe,N/A,True

10/07/14 16:44:13,N/A,C:\ProgramData\Avira\Antivirus\TEMP\SELFUPDATE\
updrgui.exe,N/A,True

04/17/15 21:03:48,N/A,C:\Program Files (x86)\Avira\AntiVir Desktop\
avwebg7.exe,N/A,True
```

Looking at the previous data, one can see that the user installed or updated Avira AntiVir on 2015-05-24 and KeePass on 2014-07-10. Also, you can find some hints that the system seems to be a virtual system as you can see the hints of Parallels, a Mac OS X virtualization platform.

If one considers the tools that have been described previously and the information that the Windows Event Log and Windows Registry contain, it is clear that in a forensic investigation, not all questions concerning a system can be answered without these sources of information.

Implementing Linux specific checks

In this section, we will describe how to implement some integrity checks to support the finding signs of system manipulation in Linux and similar (for example, BSD) systems.

These checks include the following:

- Searching for anomalies in the local user management

- Understanding and analyzing file metadata for special permissions and privileges

- Using clustering algorithms on file metadata to get indicators on where to look deeper

Checking the integrity of local user credentials

The information about local users in Linux is mostly stored in two files: /etc/passwd and /etc/shadow. The latter is optional and all the information about local users – including the hashed password – was originally stored in /etc/passwd. Soon, it was considered a security issue to store the password information in a file that is readable by every user. Therefore, the password hashes in /etc/passwd were replaced by a single x denoting that the corresponding password hash has to be looked up in /etc/shadow.

The side effect of this evolutionary process is that the password hashes in /etc/passwd are still supported and all the settings in /etc/passwd may override the credentials in /etc/shadow.

Both files are text files with one entry per line. An entry consists of multiple fields separated by colons.

The format of /etc/passwd is as follows:

- **username**: This field contains the human-readable username. It is not required for the username to be unique. However, most user management tools enforce unique usernames.

- **password hash**: This field contains the password in an encoded form according to the Posix crypt() function. If this field is empty, then the corresponding user does not require a password to log on to the system. If this field contains a value that cannot be generated by the hash algorithm, for example, an exclamation mark, then the user cannot log on using a password. However, this condition does not render the account useless. A user with a locked password can still log on using other authentication mechanisms, for example, SSH keys.

  As mentioned earlier, the special value x means that the password hash has to be found in the shadow file.

Starting with the system library `glibc2`, the `crypt()` function supports multiple hash algorithms. In that case, the password hash has the following format:

`$id$salt$encrypted`

The ID designates the hash algorithm that has been used to encode the password, for example, 1 for md5, 5 for sha256, and 6 for sha512. The salt is a randomly generated string in order to modify the hash algorithm. Consequently, even identical passwords result in different hash sums. The subfield "encrypted" holds the actual hash of the password (modified by the influence of the salt).

- **numerical user ID**: This field denotes the ID of the user. Internally, the Linux kernel uses only this numerical ID. The special ID 0 is assigned to the administrative root user. Per default, user ID 0 is granted unlimited privileges on the system.

- **numerical group ID**: This field refers to the primary group of the user.

- **comment field**: This field can contain the arbitrary information about the user and is mostly used to hold the full name of the user. Sometimes, it also contains a comma-separated list of the full username, phone number, and so on

- **user home directory**: The user home directory is a directory on the system's file system. After logging on, new processes are started with this directory as the working directory.

- **default command shell**: This optional field denotes the default shell that is to be started after a successful logon.

The format of `/etc/shadow` is as follows:

- The **username** field links the entry to the `passwd` entry with the same username.

- The **password hash** field contains the encoded password in the same format as described for the `passwd` file.

- The next five fields contain the information about the password aging, such as the date of the last password change, minimum password age, maximum password age, password warning period, and password inactivity period.

- If the **account expiration date** field is nonempty, it will be interpreted as the account expiration date. This date is expressed in days since January 1st, 1970.

With this format description, a small Python routine is sufficient to parse the file into a list of entries, each containing a list of fields as shown in the following:

```python
def read_passwd(filename):
    """Reads entries from shadow or passwd files and
        returns the content as list of entries.
        Every entry is a list of fields."""

    content = []
    with open(filename, 'r') as f:
        for line in f:
            entry = line.strip().split(':')
            content.append(entry)

    return content
```

On using this routine, typical manipulations in these files may be detected.

The first manipulation technique that we want to describe is the creation of *multiple users who share the same numerical id*. This technique can be used by attackers to plant a backdoor into the system. By creating an additional user for an existing ID, an attacker can create an alias with a separate password. The legitimate account owner would not be aware that there is an additional combination of username/password to log in to the account.

A small Python routine can detect this kind of manipulation, as follows:

```python
def detect_aliases(passwd):
    """Prints users who share a user id on the console

        Arguments:
        passwd -- contents of /etc/passwd as read by read_passwd"""

    id2user = {}
    for entry in passwd:
        username = entry[0]
        uid = entry[2]
        if uid in id2user:
            print 'User "%s" is an alias for "%s" with uid=%s' %
(username, id2user[uid], uid)
        else:
            id2user[uid] = username
```

During normal operation, the information in /etc/passwd and /etc/shadow is synced, that is, every user should appear in both the files. If there *are users appearing in only one of these files*, it is an indicator that the user management of the operating system has been bypassed. A manipulation like this can be detected with a similar script:

```
def detect_missing_users(passwd, shadow):
    """Prints users of /etc/passwd missing in /etc/shadow
       and vice versa.

       Arguments:
       passwd -- contents of /etc/passwd as read by read_passwd
       shadow -- contents of /etc/shadow as read by read_passwd"""

    passwd_users = set([e[0] for e in passwd])
    shadow_users = set([e[0] for e in shadow])

    missing_in_passwd = shadow_users - passwd_users
    if len(missing_in_passwd) > 0:
        print 'Users missing in passwd: %s' % ', '.join(missing_in_
passwd)

    missing_in_shadow = passwd_users - shadow_users
    if len(missing_in_shadow) > 0:
        print 'Users missing in shadow: %s' % ', '.join(missing_in_
shadow)
```

Just like the first function, this function should not produce any output on a normal system. If there is an output similar to Users missing in shadow: backdoor then there is a user account "backdoor" in the system without a record in the shadow file.

Users without a password should not exist in a normal system. Furthermore, all the password hashes should reside in the shadow file and all entries in the passwd file should refer to the corresponding shadow entry. The following script detects deviations from this rule:

```
def detect_unshadowed(passwd, shadow):
    """Prints users who are not using shadowing or have no password
set

       Arguments:
       passwd -- contents of /etc/passwd as read by read_passwd
       shadow -- contents of /etc/shadow as read by read_passwd"""


    nopass = [e[0] for e in passwd if e[1]=='']
```

```
nopass.extend([e[0] for e in shadow if e[1]==''])
if len(nopass) > 0:
    print 'Users without password: %s' % ', '.join(nopass)

unshadowed = [e[0] for e in passwd if e[1] != 'x' and e[1] != '']
if len(unshadowed) > 0:
    print 'Users not using password-shadowing: %s' % \
            ', '.join(unshadowed)
```

Our last example of bypassing the operating system in the creation and manipulation of user accounts is the *detection of non-standard hash algorithms* and *reusing salts for multiple user accounts*. While a Linux system allows specifying the hash algorithm for every entry in the shadow file, normally all user passwords are hashed using the same algorithm. A deviating algorithm is a signal for an entry being written to the shadow file without using the operating system tools, meaning, system manipulation. If a salt is reused across multiple password hashes, then the salt is either hardcoded into a manipulation tool or the cryptographic routines of the system have been compromised, for example, by manipulating the entropy source of the salt generation.

The following Python script is capable of detecting this kind of manipulation:

```
import re
def detect_deviating_hashing(shadow):
    """Prints users with non-standard hash methods for passwords

    Arguments:
    shadow -- contents of /etc/shadow as read by read_passwd"""

    noalgo = set()
    salt2user = {}
    algorithms = set()
    for entry in shadow:
        pwhash = entry[1]
        if len(pwhash) < 3:
            continue

        m = re.search(r'^\$([^$]{1,2})\$([^$]+)\$', pwhash)
        if not m:
            noalgo.add(entry[0])
            continue

        algo = m.group(1)
        salt = m.group(2)

        if salt in salt2user:
```

```
                    print 'Users "%s" and "%s" share same password salt "%s"'
% \
                        (salt2user[salt], entry[0], salt)
            else:
                salt2user[salt] = entry[0]

            algorithms.add(algo)

    if len(algorithms) > 1:
        print 'Multiple hashing algorithms found: %s' % ',
'.join(algorithms)

    if len(noalgo) > 0:
        print 'Users without hash algorithm spec. found: %s' % \
            ', '.join(noalgo)
```

Regular expressions

The last example uses the `re` module for **regular expression** matching to extract the algorithm specification and salt from the password hash. Regular expressions provide a fast and powerful way of text searching, matching, splitting, and replacing. Therefore, we highly recommend getting familiar with regular expressions. The documentation of the `re` module is available online at `https://docs.python.org/2/library/re.html`. The book *Mastering Python Regular Expressions*, *Felix Lopez* and *Victor Romero, Packt Publishing* provides further insights and examples on how to use regular expressions.

All of the detection methods in this section are examples of anomaly detection methods. Depending on the system environment, more specific anomaly detections can be used and implemented by following the schema of the examples. For example, on a server system, the number of users having a password set should be small. Therefore, counting all the users with passwords can be a reasonable step in the analysis of such systems.

Analyzing file meta information

In this section, we will discuss file meta information and provide examples on how it can be used in forensic analysis.

Understanding inode

Linux systems store file meta information in structures called **inodes** (**index nodes**). In a Linux filesystem, every object is represented by an inode. The data stored per inode depends on the actual filesystem type. Typical contents of an inode are as follows:

- The **index number** is the identifier of an inode. The index number is unique per file system. If two files share the same index number, then these files are **hard-linked**. Consequently, hard-linked files only differ in their filename and always have the same contents as well as the same meta information.

- The **file owner** is defined by the numerical ID of the user (UID). There can be only one owner per file. The user IDs should correspond to the entries in /etc/passwd. However, it is not guaranteed that there are only files with existing entries in /etc/passwd. Files can be transferred to the nonexisting users with administrative privileges. Furthermore, the owner of the file may have been removed from the system, making the file orphaned. For files on transportable media, for example, USB drives, there is no mechanism of mapping the user ID from one system to another. Consequently, the file owner seems to change when a USB drive is attached to a new system with different /etc/passwd. Furthermore, this can also lead to orphaned files if a UID does not exist on the system where the USB drive is attached.

- The **file group** is defined by the numerical ID of the corresponding group (GID). A file is always assigned to exactly one group. All groups of a system should be defined in /etc/groups. However, files with group IDs that are not listed in /etc/groups may exist. This indicates that the corresponding group has been deleted from the system, the medium has been transferred from another system where that group exists, or a user with administrative privileges reassigned the file to a nonexisting group.

- The **file mode (also known as "protection bits")** defines a simple form of access rights to the corresponding file. It is a bit mask defining the access rights for the file owner, for users belonging to the group that the file is assigned to, and for all other users. For each of these cases, the following bits are defined:
    - **read (r)**: If this bit is set on a regular file, the affected user is allowed to read the file contents. If the bit is set on a directory, the affected user is allowed to list the names of the contents of the directory. The read access does not include the meta-information, which is the inode data of the directory entries. Consequently, the read permission to a directory is not sufficient to read files in that directory as this would require access to the file's inode data.

      ○ **write (w)**: If this bit is set on a regular file, the affected user is allowed to modify the contents of the file in arbitrary ways including manipulation and deletion of the content. If this bit is set on a directory entry, then the affected user is allowed to create, remove, and rename the entries in that directory. The existing files in the directory have their own protection bits that define their access rights.

      ○ **execute (x)**: For regular files, this allows the affected user to start the file as a program. If the file is a compiled binary, for example, in the ELF format, then the execute privileges are sufficient to run the program. If the file is a script that has to be interpreted, then read permission (r) is also required to run the script. The reason is that the Linux kernel determines how to load the program. If it detects that the file contains a script, it loads the script interpreter with the current user's privileges. For directories, this flag grants permission to read the meta-information of the directory contents, except the names of the entries. Therefore, this allows the affected user to change the working directory to this directory.

      ○ **sticky (t)**: This bit exists only once per inode. When it is set on directories, it limits the right to delete and rename entries to the user owning the entry. On regular files, this flag is ignored or has a file system specific effect. When set on executables, this flag is used to prevent the resulting process from being swapped out from RAM. However, this purpose of the sticky bit is deprecated and Linux systems do not obey the sticky bit on executables.

      ○ **set id on execution (s)**: This bit exists for the user and for the group. When set for the user (SUID bit) on an executable file, the corresponding file is always run with its owner as the effective user. Therefore, the program is run with the privileges of the user owning the executable that is independent from the user that is actually starting the program. If the file is owned by the root user (UID 0), then the executable always runs with unlimited privileges. When the bit is set for the group (SGID bit), the executable is always started with the group of the file as effective group.

- The size of the file in bytes.
- The number of blocks that are allocated for that file.
- A timestamp denoting the last change of the file content (**mtime**).

- A timestamp denoting the last read access to the file content (**atime**).

  Access time stamp tracking can be disabled by the mount option **noatime** to limit write access to the media (for example, to extend the lifetime of the SD cards). Furthermore, read-only access (mount option **ro**) to the file system prevents atime tracking. Therefore, before analysis of atime information, it should be checked whether atime tracking was enabled for that file system. The corresponding initial mount options can be found in /etc/fstab.

- A timestamp denoting the last change of the inode data (**ctime**).

Notable extensions to these standard entries are **POSIX Access Control Lists (POSIX ACLs)**. These access control lists are supported by the major Linux file systems and allow specifying additional access entries besides the three classes (user, group, and others). These entries allow defining the additional access rights (the previously listed bits r, w and x) for additional users and groups. Evaluating POSIX ACLs will be discussed in detail in a separate section.

Another extension consists of the specification of **capability flags** to an executable. This is used for a more granular specification of privileges than using the SUID bit. Instead of giving an executable owned by the root user the SUID bit and allowing it unlimited privileges, a set of required privileges can be specified. Capabilities will also be handled in detail in a separate section.

Reading basic file metadata with Python

Python provides built-in functionality to read the file status information with the os module. The standard function to retrieve metadata from a file that is specified by its name is os.lstat(). In contrast to the more commonly used os.stat(), this function does not evaluate the targets of symbolic links but retrieves the information about the link itself. Therefore, it is not prone to run into infinite loops that are caused by circular symbolic links. Furthermore, it does not cause any errors on links that lack the link target.

The resulting object is platform dependent; however, the following information is always available: st_mode (protection bits), st_ino (inode number), st_dev (identifier of the device containing the file system object), st_nlink (number of hard links), st_uid (user ID of owner), st_gid (group ID of owner), st_size (file size in bytes), st_mtime (last modification), st_atime (last read access), st_ctime (last inode change). This information corresponds to the inode data that is described in the previous section.

A detailed description about os.stat() and os.lstat() is available at https://docs.python.org/2/library/ os.html#os.stat. This also includes the examples of platform-dependent attributes.

The st_mtime, st_atime, and st_ctime time stamps are specified in the Unix timestamp format, that is, the number of seconds since January 1st 1970. With the datetime module, this time format can be converted into a human readable form, using the following script:

```python
from datetime import datetime as dt
from os import lstat

stat_info = lstat('/etc/passwd')

atime = dt.utcfromtimestamp(stat_info.st_atime)
mtime = dt.utcfromtimestamp(stat_info.st_mtime)
ctime = dt.utcfromtimestamp(stat_info.st_ctime)

print 'File mode bits:       %s' % oct(stat_info.st_mode)
print 'Inode number:         %d' % stat_info.st_ino
print '# of hard links:      %d' % stat_info.st_nlink
print 'Owner UID:            %d' % stat_info.st_uid
print 'Group GID:            %d' % stat_info.st_gid
print 'File size (bytes)     %d' % stat_info.st_size
print 'Last read (atime)     %s' % atime.isoformat(' ')
print 'Last write (mtime)    %s' % mtime.isoformat(' ')
print 'Inode change (ctime) %s' % ctime.isoformat(' ')
```

This code listing outputs the common return values of the lstat call. A typical output looks similar to the following:

```
File mode bits:       0100644
Inode number:         1054080
# of hard links:      1
Owner UID:            0
Group GID:            0
File size (bytes)     2272
Last read (atime)     2015-05-15 09:25:15.991190
Last write (mtime)    2014-09-20 10:40:46.389162
Inode change (ctime) 2014-09-20 10:40:46.393162
```

This sample output denotes that on the lab system, /etc/passwd is a regular file with read permission for all users. This information is derived from the st_mode member of the result. On using Python's oct() function, it is converted in its octal representation, that is, *one decimal digit of the output represents exactly three bits of the protection bits*. The leading zero in the output is a common indicator for the octal representation.

The lower three digits (644 in the example output) always denote the access rights for the owner of the file (6 in the example), for users belonging to the group of the file (left 4 in the example), and all other users (last digit).

How to interpret the file mode bits?

In its octal form, the bit values of the three least significant digits represent the access rights for the owner, group, and other users (last digit). For every digit, the read access (r) has bit value 4, write access (w) has bit value 2, and execution (x) has bit value 1.

Therefore, in our example, the digit 6 denotes read and write access (4 + 2) for the owner of the file. Members of the group 0 and all other users only have read access (4).

The next digit from the right denotes the sticky bit (value 1), the SGID bit (value 2), and the SUID bit (value 4).

The stat module defines the constants for all bits of st_mode. Its documentation is available at https://docs.python.org/2/library/stat.html.

These constants can be used as a bit mask to retrieve information from st_mode. The earlier example could be extended to detect SGID, SUID, and sticky mode, as follows:

```
import stat

if stat.S_ISUID & stat_info.st_mode:
    print 'SUID mode set!'

if stat.S_ISGID & stat_info.st_mode:
    print 'SGID mode set!'

if stat.S_ISVTX & stat_info.st_mode:
    print 'Sticky mode set!'
```

For testing the code, you may use the example to evaluate the mode of /etc/passwd, /tmp, and /usr/bin/sudo on a standard Linux system. Typically, /tmp has the sticky flag set, /usr/bin/sudo has SUID set, and /etc/password has none of the special bits set.

The remaining bits denote the type of the file. The following file types may appear on a standard Linux filesystem:

File type	Check function in module stat	Description
regular	S_ISREG()	This is used to store arbitrary data
directory	S_ISDIR()	This is used to store lists of other files
soft link	S_ISLNK()	This references one destination file via name
character device	S_ISCHR()	This is the interface in the filesystem to access the character-oriented hardware, for example, terminals
block device	S_ISBLK()	This is the interface in the filesystem to access the block-oriented hardware, for example, disk partitions
fifo	S_ISFIFO()	This is the representation of a named, unidirectional interprocess interface in the filesystem
socket	S_ISSOCK()	This is the representation of a named, bidirectional interprocess interface in the filesystem

Hard links are not represented by a special file type but are merely multiple directory entries in the same filesystem sharing the same inode.

Unlike the tests for SGID, SUID, and sticky bit, the file type checks are implemented as functions of the stat module. These functions require the file mode bits as the parameter, for example:

```
from os import readlink,lstat
import stat

path = '/etc/rc5.d/S99rc.local'

stat_info = lstat(path)

if stat.S_ISREG(stat_info.st_mode):
    print 'File type: regular file'

if stat.S_ISDIR(stat_info.st_mode):
```

```
    print 'File type: directory'

if stat.S_ISLNK(stat_info.st_mode):
    print 'File type: symbolic link pointing to ',
    print readlink(path)
```

In this example, the `os.readlink()` function is used to extract the target filename if a symbolic link is encountered. Symbolic links may refer to an absolute path or a relative path starting from the location of the symbolic link in the filesystem. Absolute symbolic links have a target starting with the character /, that is, the target is to be searched starting with the root directory of the system.

 If you mount your copy of the evidence in your lab environment for analysis, the absolute symbolic links are either broken or they point to a file in your lab workstation! The relative symbolic links remain intact as long as their destination resides in the same partition as the link.

A possible output of the previous example code could be - `File type: symbolic link pointing to ../init.d/rc.local` - , which is an example of a relative link.

Evaluating POSIX ACLs with Python

The file mode bits, which are defined in the file's inode, only allow three addressees for permissions: the file owner, the users belonging to the file's group, and everybody else.

If a more granular set of permissions is required, the traditional solution will be to create a group that consists of all the users who should have access and transfer the file to that group. However, the creation of such groups has major disadvantages. First, the list of groups can become unnecessarily large. Second, the creation of such groups requires administrative privileges and therefore, breaks the Linux/Unix concept of **discretionary access control**.

 Discretionary access control is the concept of allowing the owner of the information, that is, the file owner, to decide who should be allowed the access. In discretionary access control, ownership is the sole requirement for being allowed to grant or revoke access to a resource.

Last but not least, file owners may just open up files and directories for everyone on the system if there is no group that is matching to the list of the users to authorize. This breaks the *concept of least privilege*, that is, not granting more permissions on a system than required for its operation.

To maintain the discretionary access control as well as the concept of least privilege, an optional extension to the file access mode was specified, that is, **POSIX ACL**. Besides allowing read, write, and execute permissions for the file owner, group, and others, POSIX ACLs allow to specify the following:

- Specific read, write, and execute permissions for arbitrary users
- Specific read, write, and execute permissions for arbitrary groups
- Every privilege that is not set in the access mask is not granted. Only the permissions of the file owner and others are not affected by the access mask.

On the command line, the getfacl and setfacl tools can be used to read and modify the POSIX ACL entries respectively:

```
user@lab:~$ touch /tmp/mytest
user@lab:~$ getfacl /tmp/mytest
getfacl: Removing leading '/' from absolute path names
# file: tmp/mytest
# owner: user
# group: user
user::rw-
group::r--
other::r--
```

This example also shows that the standard permission set is reflected in the POSIX ACL. Consequently, if POSIX ACLs are supported on a filesystem, then the complete permission set is contained in POSIX ACLs.

Let's revoke the read access to other users and add read/write access to the user games, as shown here:

```
user@lab:~$ setfacl -m o::0 -m u:games:rw /tmp/mytest
user@lab:~$ getfacl /tmp/mytest
getfacl: Removing leading '/' from absolute path names
# file: tmp/mytest
# owner: user
# group: user
user::rw-
user:games:rw-
group::r--
mask::rw-
```

```
other::---
user@lab:~$ ls -l /tmp/mytest
-rw-rw----+ 1 user user 0 May 16 16:59 /tmp/mytest
```

The -m o::0 parameter removes all the privileges from other users while
–m u:games:rw grants read/write access to the user games. The subsequent call
to getfacls shows the additional entry for user:games and the changed entry for
other. Furthermore, a mask entry is automatically created to limit the access from
all the listed groups and users (except the file owner) to read/write.

The output of the ls command shows a plus sign + to indicate the existence of
the additional ACL entries. As also indicated by the output of ls, tools that only
evaluate the mode bits of a file are unaware of the additional permissions, for
example, the additional access privileges for the user games do not show up in the
standard output of ls or other file management applications.

Forensic tools that do not look for and interpret POSIX
ACL entries may miss the additional access rights that are
introduced by the ACL entries! Consequently, the investigator
may get a false impression of strict, effective privileges.

Fortunately, the Python library **pylibacl** can be used to read and evaluate POSIX
ACLs and hence, avoid that pitfall. The library introduces the posix1e module,
that is, a reference to the initial draft first mentioning POSIX ACLs. The detailed
documentation about this library is available at http://pylibacl.k1024.org/.

The following script is an example of how to look for files with the additional
ACL entries:

```
#!/usr/bin/env python

import os
from os.path import join
import posix1e
import re
import stat
import sys


def acls_from_file(filename, include_standard = False):
    """Returns the extended ACL entries from the given
        file as list of the text representation.

        Arguments:
        filename -- the file name to get the ACLs from
```

```
                    include_standard -- if True, ACL entries representing
                                     standard Linux permissions will be
                                     included"""
        result = []
        try:
            acl = posix1e.ACL(file=filename)
        except:
            print 'Error getting ACLs from %s' % filename
            return []

        text = acl.to_any_text(options=posix1e.TEXT_ABBREVIATE | posix1e.
TEXT_NUMERIC_IDS)

        for entry in text.split("\n"):
            if not include_standard and \
                re.search(r'^[ugo]::', entry) != None:
                continue
            result.append(entry)

        return result


def get_acl_list(basepath, include_standard = False):
    """Collects all POSIX ACL entries of a directory tree.

    Arguments:
    basepath -- directory to start from
    include_standard -- if True, ACL entries representing
                        standard Linux permissions will be
                        included"""
    result = {}

    for root, dirs, files in os.walk(basepath):
        for f in dirs + files:
            fullname = join(root, f)

            # skip symbolic links (target ACL applies)
            if stat.S_ISLNK(os.lstat(fullname).st_mode):
                continue

            acls = acls_from_file(fullname, include_standard)
            if len(acls) > 0:
```

```
            result[fullname] = acls

        return result

if __name__ == '__main__':
    if len(sys.argv) < 2:
        print 'Usage %s root_directory' % sys.argv[0]
        sys.exit(1)

    acl_list = get_acl_list(sys.argv[1], False)

    for filename, acls in acl_list.iteritems():
        print "%s: %s" % (filename, ','.join(acls))
```

The `posix1e.ACL` class represents all the permissions set on a specific object on the filesystem. When its constructor is called with a filename as the `file` parameter, it represents ACL of that file. In the `acls_from_file()` function, a regular expression is used to detect and optionally filter out the standard permissions from the text representation of the ACL set.

The `os.walk()` function is used to iterate over a subtree of the filesystem. If you iterate over `os.walk()` like in the example, you get a triple in each iteration denoting the following:

- The currently visited directory
- A list with all of its subdirectories (relative to the currently visited directory)
- A list with all of its nondirectory entries, for example, files and soft links (relative to the currently visited directory)

The check in the last highlighted line of the script is an example of the evaluating file type information as described in the previous section. It is used to detect and skip symbolic links. The symbolic links always use ACLs of their target and consequently, POSIX ACLs on symbolic links are not supported.

When invoked with /tmp as the parameter on our lab machine, it generates the following output:

/tmp/mytest: u:5:rw-,m::rw-

This output shows that the script detected the leftovers from our first tests with POSIX ACLs: An additional read/write permission for user (u) ID 5 (that is, user `games` on the lab machine) and a mask (m) entry that limits the effective privileges to read/write. The script outputs the numerical user IDs because pylibacl would otherwise use your workstation's /etc/passwd to look up the usernames.

If you run this script on a copy of the filesystem that contains your evidence, it will list every filesystem object with permissions beyond the Linux standard permission set.

> Most standard Linux systems and their applications do not use POSIX ACLs. Therefore, if you encounter any additional POSIX ACL entries during your investigation, it is a good idea to thoroughly check whether these POSIX ACLs were the result of a legitimate and benign system operation.

Reading file capabilities with Python

Traditionally, in Linux, there are two types of administrative privileges: root and non-root. If a process is granted the root privileges, that is, it runs with UID 0, then it may bypass every security restriction of the Linux kernel. On the other hand, if a process does not run with these root privileges, then all security restrictions of the kernel apply.

In order to replace this **all or nothing** mechanism with a more fine-grained system, the **Linux capabilities** were introduced. The corresponding man page describes it as the following:

For the purpose of performing permission checks, traditional UNIX implementations distinguish two categories of processes: privileged processes (whose effective user ID is 0, referred to as superuser or root), and unprivileged processes (whose effective UID is nonzero).

Privileged processes bypass all kernel permission checks, while unprivileged processes are subject to full permission checking based on the process's credentials (usually: effective UID, effective GID, and supplementary group list).

Starting with kernel 2.2, Linux divides the privileges traditionally associated with superuser into distinct units, known as capabilities, which can be independently enabled and disabled. Capabilities are a per-thread attribute.

> **What capabilities exist?**
> The list of Linux capabilities can be found in the /usr/include/ linux/capability.h file on a standard Linux system. A more human-readable form is provided in the capabilities man page. It can be viewed via man 7 capabilities. The Linux capabilities include every special permission granted to the root user, for example, overriding file permissions, using raw network connections, and so on.

Capabilities can be assigned to the threads of processes during the execution and to the executables on the filesystem. In either case, there are always three sets of capabilities:

- **permitted set (p)**: The permitted set contains all capabilities that a thread may request. If an executable is started, its permitted set is used to initialize the permitted set of the process.

- **inheritable set (i)**: The inheritable set of an execution set defines the capabilities that may be forwarded from the thread to a child process. However, only capabilities that are defined in the inheritable set of the executable file of the child process are forwarded to the child process. Therefore, a capability is only inherited if it is in the inheritable set of the parent process and in the file attribute of the child executable.

- **effective set (e)**: This is the set of capabilities that the Linux kernel actually checks when a privileged operation is requested from an execution thread. By calling `cap_set_proc()`, a process can disable or enable the capabilities. Only capabilities in the permitted set (p) may be enabled. On the filesystem, the effective set is represented by only one bit. If this bit is set, the executable is started with all of its permitted capabilities also being effective. If the bit is not set, the new process starts without the effective capabilities.

 Capabilities grant administrative privileges to executables without requiring the SUID bit in the file mode. Therefore, during a forensic investigation, all the file capabilities should be documented.

Using Python's ctypes, the shared `libcap.so.2` library can be utilized to retrieve all the file capabilities from a directory tree, as follows:

```
#!/usr/bin/env python

import ctypes
import os
from os.path import join
import sys

# load shared library
libcap2 = ctypes.cdll.LoadLibrary('libcap.so.2')

class cap2_smart_char_p(ctypes.c_char_p):
    """Implements a smart pointer to a string allocated
       by libcap2.so.2"""
    def __del__(self):
```

```
            libcap2.cap_free(self)

    # note to ctypes: cap_to_text() returns a pointer
    # that needs automatic deallocation
    libcap2.cap_to_text.restype = cap2_smart_char_p

def caps_from_file(filename):
    """Returns the capabilities of the given file as text"""

    cap_t = libcap2.cap_get_file(filename)
    if cap_t == 0:
        return ''
    return libcap2.cap_to_text(cap_t, None).value


def get_caps_list(basepath):
    """Collects file capabilities of a directory tree.

    Arguments:
    basepath -- directory to start from"""

    result = {}
    for root, dirs, files in os.walk(basepath):
        for f in files:
            fullname = join(root, f)
            caps = caps_from_file(fullname)
            if caps != '':
                result[fullname] = caps

    return result

if __name__ == '__main__':
    if len(sys.argv) < 2:
        print 'Usage %s root_directory' % sys.argv[0]
        sys.exit(1)

    capabilities = get_caps_list(sys.argv[1])

    for filename, caps in capabilities.iteritems():
        print "%s: %s" % (filename, caps)
```

The first highlighted line loads the `libcap.so.2` library for direct use in Python. As the memory for the text representation of the capabilities is allocated in this library, it is the responsibility of the caller, that is, our script, to deallocate this memory after usage. The solution for this task, which was chosen here, is to extend the `ctype` default representation of **pointer to character**, that is, `ctype.c_char_p`. The resulting `cap2_smart_char_p` class is a simple version of the so-called **smart pointer**: If the Python representation of objects of this class is being destroyed, the objects will automatically call `cap_free()` to free the corresponding resources that are previously allocated by `libcap.so.2`.

With the `cap_get_file()` library function, the capabilities of a file can be retrieved. The subsequent call to `cap_to_text()` transforms this internal representation into human-readable text.

If the script is saved to `chap03_capabilities.py`, then it can be called on the lab machine as shown in the following:

```
user@lab:~$ python chap03_capabilities.py /usr
```

Of course, the output is highly dependent on the Linux version and distribution. It may look similar to the following:

```
/usr/bin/gnome-keyring-daemon: = cap_ipc_lock+ep
```

This output means that only one executable in `/usr` has the special capabilities set: `/usr/bin/gnome-keyring-daemon`. The name of the capability is given by the constant `cap_ipc_lock`, this capability is in the permitted set and is immediately effective on starting this program as denoted by `+ep`.

To resolve the meaning of `cap_ipc_lock`, we will call the following:

```
user@lab:~$ man 7 capabilities
```

Then we will search for CAP_IPC_LOCK. This reveals that the capability grants the right to lock the parts or all of a process memory in RAM and prevent the swapping of that process. As `gnome-keyring-daemon` stores user credentials in RAM, having the privilege to prevent these credentials from being written to the swap is highly advisable from a security perspective.

 Currently, most of the standard Linux distributions make little use of the file capability feature. Therefore, the discovered file capabilities — especially those that are not required for normal operation — may be the first indicator of system manipulation.

Clustering file information

In the previous section, we showed you how to retrieve and collect file metadata from the Linux/Unix filesystem. In this section, we will provide examples to locate the changes in the filesystem metadata, which may be interesting for further inspection by the investigator.

Creating histograms

Creating histograms is the process of clustering the data in bins of equal size and drawing the size of these bins. With Python, plotting these histograms can be easily achieved using the Python **matplotlib** module. A detailed documentation including the use cases, examples, and Python source code is available at `http://matplotlib.org/`.

The following Python script can be used to generate and display the histograms of file access times and file modification times of a directory tree:

```python
#!/usr/bin/env python

from datetime import datetime
from matplotlib.dates import DateFormatter
import matplotlib.pyplot as plt
import os
from os.path import join
import sys

# max. number of bars on the histogram
NUM_BINS = 200

def gen_filestats(basepath):
    """Collects metadata about a directory tree.

    Arguments:
    basepath -- root directory to start from

    Returns:
    Tuple with list of file names and list of
    stat results."""

    filenames = []
    filestats = []

    for root, dirs, files in os.walk(basepath):
        for f in files:
```

```
            fullname = join(root, f)
            filenames.append(fullname)
            filestats.append(os.lstat(fullname))
    return (filenames, filestats)


def show_date_histogram(times, heading='', block=False):
    """Draws and displays a histogram over the given timestamps.

    Arguments:
    times -- array of time stamps as seconds since 1970-01-01
    heading -- heading to write to the drawing
    block --- if True, the graph window waits for user interaction"""

    fig, ax = plt.subplots()

    times = map(lambda x: datetime.fromtimestamp(x).toordinal(),
times)

    ax.hist(times, NUM_BINS)
    plt.xlabel('Date')
    plt.ylabel('# of files')
    plt.title(heading)

    ax.autoscale_view()

    ax.xaxis.set_major_formatter(DateFormatter('%Y-%m-%d'))
    fig.autofmt_xdate()

    fig.show()
    if block:
        plt.show()


if __name__ == '__main__':
    if len(sys.argv) < 2:
        print 'Usage %s base_directory' % sys.argv[0]
        sys.exit(1)

    path = sys.argv[1]

    (names, stats) = gen_filestats(path)

    # extract time stamps
    mtimes = map(lambda x: x.st_mtime, stats)
```

```
atimes = map(lambda x: x.st_atime, stats)

show_date_histogram(mtimes, 'mtimes of ' + path)
show_date_histogram(atimes, 'atimes of ' + path, True)
```

The `gen_filestats()` function iterates the directory tree and collects all inode data. The `show_date_histogram()` function is used to generate and display the data as a histogram.

In the first highlighted line of the code, the encoding of the timestamp is changed. This is required because the inode data gives us the timestamps as number of seconds since 1970-01-01. This format is what `datetime.fromtimestamp()` expects. However, Matplotlib needs timestamps in number of days since 0001-01-01 of the Gregorian calendar. Fortunately, the `datetime` class can provide this representation with its `toordinal()` method.

The next highlighted line is the actual generation and drawing of the histogram in the following figure. All the other statements of `show_date_histogram()` merely serve the purpose of adding labels and formatting to the drawing.

The following is a sample result of the `/sbin` directory on a standard Linux desktop system:

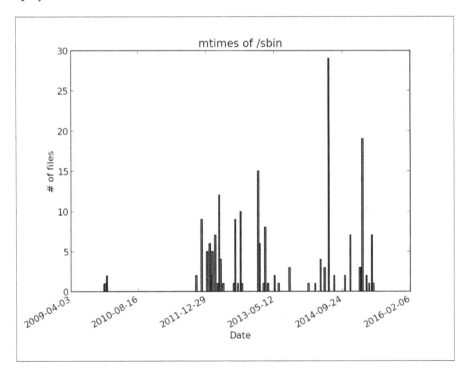

Here, the dates of the major system updates are clearly visible. An investigator should be aware that the file metadata and these histograms *do not contain historic file information*. Therefore, from the previous histogram, one cannot derive that there were little or no security updates before December 2011. It is more likely that most of the files that were patched before December 2011 have been modified later on, therefore, masking older patches in the histogram.

Let's take a look at the access time distribution of this directory:

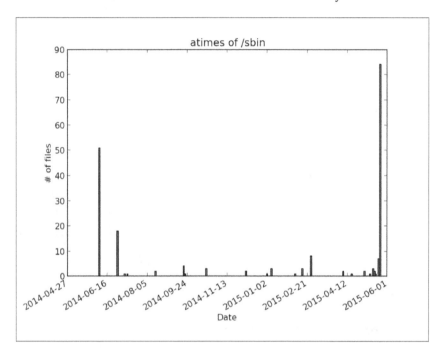

This histogram provides some insight about the access pattern of this directory. First, the atime timestamp tracking is enabled on the systems. Otherwise, no current access timestamps would be visible in the histogram. About half of the files have been read recently. This information can be used to verify the information about the time when the evidence was acquired or when the system operator claimed to have taken the system offline.

Furthermore, the contents of this directory were very likely not scanned regularly for viruses and were not recently packed into an archive. Both the actions usually update the atime timestamp.

If the following command is issued on the system, then /sbin is scanned for viruses. Of course, the scanner has to read every file in that directory to scan its contents:

```
user@lab:~$ clamscan -i /sbin
```

The atime diagram of /sbin reflects the changes, as follows:

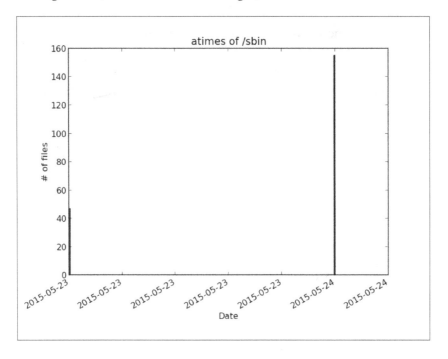

The changes are obvious: Most of the bars have collapsed in one at the current time, that is, the time of the virus scan. The timescale is stretched to a single day. Consequently, the bar on the left can also be considered to be a result of the virus scan.

If there is a directory having all the atime timestamps on a single date, then this directory was recently copied, scanned for viruses, or packed in an archive. Of course, with sufficient access rights, the timestamps could have been manually set as well.

Advanced histogram techniques

In the previous section, the histograms were used to learn about the filesystem metadata. However, these histograms have a number of disadvantages, as follows:

- All histogram bars are of equal width

- The bars are not placed according to the actual clustering of the data, for example, a cluster may be distributed over two bars

- The outliers disappear, that is, the low bars are easily confused with the empty bars

Therefore, this section presents an example of how to use simple **machine learning algorithms** for a smarter clustering of the data. A widely used machine learning library for Python is **scikit-learn**. Among other domains, it provides several algorithms for clustering the input data. We recommend visiting http://scikit-learn.org for an overview of all the algorithms and examples of their use. The following Python script uses the DBSCAN algorithm from scikit-learn to generate clusters of a given width (in days):

```
#!/usr/bin/python

from datetime import date
import numpy as np
import os
from os.path import join
from sklearn.cluster import DBSCAN
import sys

def gen_filestats(basepath):
    """Collects metadata about a directory tree.

    Arguments:
    basepath -- root directory to start from

    Returns:
    Tuple with list of file names and list of
    stat results."""

    filenames = []
    filestats = []

    for root, dirs, files in os.walk(basepath):
        for f in files:
```

```
                    fullname = join(root, f)
                    filenames.append(fullname)
                    filestats.append(os.lstat(fullname))
            return (filenames, filestats)



    def _calc_clusters(data, eps, minsamples):
        samples = np.array(data)
        db = DBSCAN(eps=eps, min_samples=minsamples).fit(samples)
        return (db.labels_, db.core_sample_indices_)

    def calc_atime_clusters(stats, days=1, mincluster=5):
        """Clusters files regarding to their 'last access' date.

        Arguments:
        stats -- file metadata as returned as 2nd element by gen_filestats
        days  -- approx. size of a cluster (default: accessed on same day)
        mincluster -- min. number of files to make a new cluster

        Returns:
        Tuple with array denoting cluster membership
        and indexes of representatives of cluster cores"""

        atimes = map(lambda x: [x.st_atime], stats)
        return _calc_clusters(atimes, days * 24 * 3600, mincluster)

    def calc_mtime_clusters(stats, days=1, mincluster=5):
        """Clusters files regarding to their 'last modified' date.

        Arguments:
        stats -- file metadata as returned as 2nd element by gen_filestats
        days  -- approx. size of a cluster (default: accessed on same day)
        mincluster -- min. number of files to make a new cluster

        Returns:
        Tuple with array denoting cluster membership
        and indexes of representatives of cluster cores"""

        mtimes = map(lambda x: [x.st_mtime], stats)
        return _calc_clusters(mtimes, days * 24 * 3600, mincluster)


    def calc_histogram(labels, core_indexes, timestamps):
```

```
    # reserve space for outliers (label -1), even if there are none
    num_entries = len(set(labels)) if -1 in labels else
len(set(labels))+1

    counters = [0] * num_entries
    coredates = [0] * num_entries

    for c in core_indexes:
        i = int(c)
        coredates[int(labels[i])+1] = timestamps[i]

    for l in labels:
        counters[int(l)+1] += 1

    return zip(coredates, counters)

def print_histogram(histogram):
    # sort histogram by core time stamps
    sort_histo = sorted(histogram, cmp=lambda x,y: cmp(x[0],y[0]))

    print '[date around] [number of files]'
    for h in sort_histo:
        if h[0] == 0:
            print '<outliers>',
        else:
            t = date.fromtimestamp(h[0]).isoformat()
            print t,
        print '    %6d' % h[1]



if __name__ == '__main__':
    if len(sys.argv) < 2:
        print 'Usage %s base_directory [number of days in one
cluster]' % sys.argv[0]
        sys.exit(1)

    days = 1
    if len(sys.argv) > 2:
        days = int(sys.argv[2])

    names, stats = gen_filestats(sys.argv[1])

    print '%d files to analyze...' % len(names)
```

```
atime_labels, atime_cores = calc_atime_clusters(stats, days)
mtime_labels, mtime_cores = calc_mtime_clusters(stats, days)

atimes = map(lambda x: x.st_atime, stats)
mtimes = map(lambda x: x.st_mtime, stats)

ahisto = calc_histogram(atime_labels, atime_cores, atimes)
mhisto = calc_histogram(mtime_labels, mtime_cores, mtimes)

print "\n=== Access time histogram ==="
print_histogram(ahisto)

print "\n=== Modification time histogram ==="
print_histogram(mhisto)
```

The `gen_filestats()` function is identical to the version used for the basic histograms in the previous section. The `calc_atime_clusters()` and `calc_mtime_clusters()` functions extract the access and modification time of the collected information and pass it on to the cluster generation in `_calc_clusters`. The DBSCAN is initialized with two parameters: the size of a cluster (`eps`, in seconds) and the minimum number of sample data that can make a cluster (`min_samples`). After the parameters of the algorithm are set, the data is fed in for the purpose of clustering via the `fit()` method.

The result of this clustering is a tuple that consists of **labels** and a list of indices per label. A label correlates to a cluster that is found in the input data. Its value is the center, that is, the average date, of all dates of the cluster. The special label `-1` acts as a container for all the outliers, that is, all the data that could not be assigned to a cluster.

The `calc_histogram()` function counts the size of each cluster and returns the histogram, that is, the labels and the number of entries as two-dimensional array.

We can run this Python script on the `/sbin` directory, as follows:

user@lab:~$ python timecluster.py /sbin

The output may look similar to the following:

202 files to analyze...

=== Access time histogram ===

```
[date around]  [number of files]
<outliers>              0
2015-05-24            202


=== Modification time histogram ===
[date around]  [number of files]
<outliers>             64
2011-11-20              9
2012-02-09              5
2012-03-02              6
2012-03-31             11
2012-07-26              6
2012-09-11             10
2013-01-18             15
2013-01-26              6
2013-03-07              8
2014-06-18             29
2014-11-20              7
2015-02-16             19
2015-05-01              7
```

Here, the access time histogram shows only one entry, reflecting our previous scan of the directory. Furthermore, all the major system updates in the recent past are shown in the modification time histogram.

With this tool, the investigator is able to cluster the filesystem information in order to detect the scanning or extraction of the directories as well as the neglected security patches. Furthermore, the special cluster -1 can be analyzed to get the names of the files, which were modified outside of the major system updates.

Summary

In this chapter, we saw prominent examples of the special properties of Microsoft Windows and Linux (and Linux-like) systems. You are now able to extract information from the Windows event log, the Windows registry, Linux files, and the Linux filesystem. Using Python, all of this information can be automatically and semiautomatically analyzed for the Indicators of Compromise, reconstructing the recent system activity, and signs of exfiltration.

Furthermore, reading the filesystem capabilities shows us how to use ctype to load the native libraries to assist the filesystem analysis.

In the clustering of file information, we provided the first example on how to use the basic machine learning algorithms to support the forensic analysis.

Now that we took a look at the local systems, we will go to the next chapter and take a look at the network traffic and how to search for the Indicators of Compromise (IOC) there.

4
Using Python for
Network Forensics

In this chapter, we will focus on the parts of the forensic investigation that are specific to the network layer. We will choose one of the most widely used Python packages for the purpose of manipulating and analyzing network traffic (**Scapy**) as well as a newly released open source framework by the U.S. Army Research Laboratory (**Dshell**). For both the toolkits, we have selected the examples of interesting evidence. This chapter will teach you the following:

- How to search for IOC in network traffic
- How to extract files for further analysis
- How to monitor accessed files through **Server Message Block** (**SMB**)
- How to build your own port scanner

Using Dshell during an investigation

Dshell is a Python-based network forensic analysis toolkit that is developed by the U.S. Army Research Laboratory and released as open source at the end of 2014. It can help in making the forensic investigations on the network layer a little easier. The toolkit comes with a large number of decoders that can be used out of the box and are very helpful. Some of these decoders are as follows:

- **dns**: Extracts and summarizes DNS queries/responses
- **reservedips**: Identifies the DNS resolutions that fall in the reserved IP space
- **large-flows**: Displays the netflows that have at least transferred 1MB

- **rip-http**: Extracts the files from the HTTP traffic
- **protocols**: Identifies non-standard protocols
- **synrst**: Detects failed attempts to connect (SYN followed by a RST/ACK)

Dshell can be installed in our lab environment by cloning the sources from GitHub at, `https://github.com/USArmyResearchLab/Dshell` and running `install-ubuntu.py`. This script will automatically download the missing packages and build the executables that we will need afterwards. Dshell can be used against the pcap files that have been recorded during the incidents or as a result of an IDS alert. A **packet capture (pcap)** file is either created by libpcap (on Linux) or WinPcap (on Windows).

In the following section, we will explain how an investigator can make use of Dshell by demonstrating the toolkit with real-world scenarios that are gathered from `http://malware-traffic-analysis.net`.

The first example is a malicious ZIP file that a user has encountered through an email link. The user logged in to Gmail and clicked the download link in the mail. This can easily be seen with the web decoder of Dshell, as follows:

```
user@lab:~$ source labenv/bin/activate

(labenv)user@lab:~$ ./dshell


(labenv)user@lab:~$ Dshell> decode -d web infected_email.pcap


web 2015-05-29 16:23:44     10.3.162.105:62588 ->   74.125.226.181:80
** GET mail.google.com/ HTTP/1.1
// 200 OK  2015-05-29 14:23:40 **


web 2015-05-29 16:24:15     10.3.162.105:62612 <-   149.3.144.218:80
** GET sciclubtermeeuganee.it/wp-content/plugins/feedweb_data/pdf_efax_
message_3537462.zip HTTP/1.1
// 200 OK  2015-05-28 14:00:22 **
```

When looking at the previous traffic extract, the ZIP file could be the first Indicator of Compromise. Therefore, we should take a deeper look at it. The easiest way to do this is to rip the ZIP file out of the pcap file and compare its md5 hash against the VirusTotal database:

```
(labenv)user@lab:~$ Dshell> decode -d rip-http --bpf "tcp and port 62612"
infected_email.pcap


rip-http 2015-05-29 16:24:15      10.3.162.105:62612 <-
149.3.144.218:80    ** New file: pdf_efax_message_3537462.zip
(sciclubtermeeuganee.it/wp-content/plugins/feedweb_data/pdf_efax_
message_3537462.zip) **
 --> Range: 0 - 132565
rip-http 2015-05-29 16:24:15      10.3.162.105:62612 <-
149.3.144.218:80    ** File done: ./pdf_efax_message_3537462.zip
(sciclubtermeeuganee.it/wp-content/plugins/feedweb_data/pdf_efax_
message_3537462.zip) **


(labenv)user@lab:~$ Dshell> md5sum pdf_efax_message_3537462.zip

9cda66cba36af799c564b8b33c390bf4  pdf_efax_message_3537462.zip
```

In this simple case, our first guess was right as the downloaded ZIP file contains another executable that part of an infostealer malware kit, as seen in the following screenshot:

Another really good example is searching for the accessed files on a network share via the SMB protocol. This can be very helpful when trying to find out whether an attacker was able to access or even exfiltrate the data and — if successful — which data has been potentially leaked:

```
(labenv)user@lab:~$ Dshell> decode -d smbfiles exfiltration.pcap


smbfiles 2005-11-19 04:31:58     192.168.114.1:52704 ->
192.168.114.129:445    ** VNET3\administrator \\192.168.114.129\TEST\
torture_qfileinfo.txt (W) **

smbfiles 2005-11-19 04:31:58     192.168.114.1:52704 ->
192.168.114.129:445    ** VNET3\administrator \\192.168.114.129\
TESTTORTUR~1.TXT (-) **

smbfiles 2005-11-19 04:31:58     192.168.114.1:52705 ->
192.168.114.129:445    ** VNET3\administrator \\192.168.114.129\TEST\
testsfileinfo\fname_test_18.txt (W) **
```

With the help of the **rip-smb-uploads** decoder, Dshell is also able to automatically extract all the uploaded files of the recorded pcap file. Another interesting example is searching for the IOC with the help of the snort rules, which can also be done by Dshell, as follows:

```
(labenv)user@lab:~$ Dshell> decode -d snort malicious-word-document.
pcap --snort_rule 'alert tcp any 443 -> any any (msg:"ET CURRENT_EVENTS
Tor2Web .onion Proxy Service SSL Cert (1)"; content:"|55 04 03|";
content:"*.tor2web.";)' -snort_alert


snort 2015-02-03 01:58:26     38.229.70.4:443    --
192.168.120.154:50195 ** ET CURRENT_EVENTS Tor2Web .onion Proxy Service
SSL Cert (1) **

snort 2015-02-03 01:58:29     38.229.70.4:443    --
192.168.120.154:50202 ** ET CURRENT_EVENTS Tor2Web .onion Proxy Service
SSL Cert (1) **

snort 2015-02-03 01:58:32     38.229.70.4:443    --
192.168.120.154:50204 ** ET CURRENT_EVENTS Tor2Web .onion Proxy Service
SSL Cert (1) **
```

In this example we opened a potentially malicious Word document that we have received within a spam email. The Word document is trying to download the **Vawtrak** malware and thereby communicating over the **Tor** network. The snort rule we are using originates from Emerging Threats, (refer to http://www. emergingthreats.net/), and is searching for known SSL certificates for the **Tor2Web** service (a service to let users access **Tor Onion Services** without using the Tor Browser). Similar checks can be done using all available snort rules and can be very helpful if you are searching for a specific attack within the network.

As an alternative to the shown pcap files, all the demonstrated examples can also be run against an active network connection with the help of the `-i interface_name` flag as shown in the following:

```
(labenv)user@lab:~$ Dshell> decode -d netflow -i eth0

2015-05-15 21:35:31.843922    192.168.161.131 ->    85.239.127.88  (None
-> None)  TCP    52007     80    0     0         0         0  5.1671s

2015-05-15 21:35:31.815329    192.168.161.131 ->    85.239.127.84  (None
-> None)  TCP    46664     80    0     0         0         0  5.1976s

2015-05-15 21:35:32.026244    192.168.161.131 ->    208.91.198.88  (None
-> None)  TCP    40595     80    9    25      4797    169277  6.5642s

2015-05-15 21:35:33.562660    192.168.161.131 ->    208.91.198.88  (None
-> None)  TCP    40599     80    9    19      4740     85732  5.2030s

2015-05-15 21:35:32.026409    192.168.161.131 ->    208.91.198.88  (None
-> None)  TCP    40596     80    7     8      3843    121616  6.7580s

2015-05-15 21:35:33.559826    192.168.161.131 ->    208.91.198.88  (None
-> None)  TCP    40597     80    5    56      2564    229836  5.2732s
```

In this example, we are generating the netflow data of an active connection. Dshell is purely written in Python, which makes it highly adaptable to all the needs of the forensic investigators and can also be used in a chain with other tools or predefined processes.

If you want to test this, you can download the sample files from http://www.emergingthreats.net/.

Using Scapy during an investigation

Another great Python-based tool to analyze and manipulate the network traffic is **Scapy**. According to the developer website, http://www.secdev.org/projects/scapy/:

> *"Scapy is a powerful interactive packet manipulation program. It is able to forge or decode packets of a wide number of protocols, send them on the wire, capture them, match requests and replies, and much more."*

Scapy differs from the standard tools (and also from Dshell) by providing an investigator with the ability to write small Python scripts that can manipulate or analyze the network traffic—either in a recorded form or in real-time. Furthermore, Scapy has the ability to perform deep packet dissection, passive OS fingerprinting, or plotting via third-party tools, such as **GnuPlot**, as built-in features are already available.

The following Python script, which is taken from *Grow Your Own Forensic Tools:
A Taxonomy of Python Libraries Helpful for Forensic Analysis, SANS Institute InfoSec
Reading Room,* is a very brief example of how powerful Scapy is:

```
import scapy, GeoIP
from scapy import *

geoIp = GeoIP.new(GeoIP.GEOIP_MEMORY_CACHE)
def locatePackage(pkg):
  src=pkg.getlayer(IP).src
  dst=pkg.getlayer(IP).dst
  srcCountry = geoIp.country_code_by_addr(src)
  dstCountry = geoIp.country_code_by_addr(dst)
  print src+"("+srcCountry+") >> "+dst+"("+dstCountry+")\n"
try:
  while True:
    sniff(filter="ip", prn=locatePackage, store=0)
except KeyboardInterrupt:
  print "\n" + "Scan Aborted!"
```

This script records the statistics about the geolocation of the IP address source and the
destination of an ongoing network connection. After importing the Scapy package
into our Python script, we call the sniff function and use a filter to detect only the IP
packets. The last parameter in the sniff function is very important if you plan to run
Scapy scripts for a long time. With the help of the store parameter, you can tell Scapy
to not cache all the packages in RAM during the runtime and thus make the script
faster and resource saving. The subsequent function looks up the geolocation of the
source and destination IP address that is extracted from each packet.

In the next example, we will illustrate how to build a very simple port scanner with
the help of Scapy, as follows:

```
#!/usr/bin/env python

import sys
from scapy.all import *

targetRange = sys.argv[1]
targetPort = sys.argv[2]
conf.verb=0

p=IP(dst=targetRange)/TCP(dport=int(targetPort), flags="S")
ans,unans=sr(p, timeout=9)

for answers in ans:
        if answers[1].flags == 2:
                print answers[1].src
```

This small script is able to scan whole IP ranges for a given open port. If you are searching the web servers that are listening on port 80, you can use the script, as follows:

```
(labenv)user@lab:~$ ./scanner.py 192.168.161.1/24 80
WARNING: No route found for IPv6 destination :: (no default route?)
Begin emission:..........
192.168.161.12
192.168.161.34
192.168.161.111

....
```

We can also use the **Address Resolution Protocol (ARP)** for a reconnaissance of the whole network range that our system is connected to. With the help of the following script, we get a nicely printed table with all the IP addresses that are online and also their corresponding MAC addresses:

```python
#! /usr/bin/env python

import sys
from scapy.all import srp,Ether,ARP,conf

if len(sys.argv) != 2:
        print "Usage: arp_ping <net> (e.g.,: arp_ping 192.168.1.0/24)"
        sys.exit(1)

conf.verb=0
ans,unans=srp(Ether(dst="ff:ff:ff:ff:ff:ff")/ARP(pdst=sys.argv[1]),
timeout=9)

print r"+------------------+-----------------+"
print r"|       MAC        |       IP        |"
print r"+------------------+-----------------+"
for snd,rcv in ans:
        print rcv.sprintf(r" %Ether.src% | %ARP.psrc%")
print r"+------------------+-----------------+"
```

When executing the script, we will receive something similar to this:

```
(labenv)user@lab:~$ ./arp_ping.py 192.168.161.131/24
WARNING: No route found for IPv6 destination :: (no default route?)
```

```
+------------------+------------------+
|       MAC        |        IP        |
+------------------+------------------+
 00:50:56:c0:00:08 | 192.168.161.1
 00:50:56:f5:d3:83 | 192.168.161.2
 00:50:56:f1:2d:28 | 192.168.161.254
+------------------+------------------+
```

Scripts such as these two can be very useful if no port scanner is available on the system or if you want to chain a port scanner with the other Python-based scripts for your investigation.

Summary

This chapter provided an overview of the domains of network-based forensic investigations and the examples with Dshell and Scapy. We have demonstrated how to search for suspicious HTTP connections (such as file downloads) or how to search for leaked data through the SMB protocol with Dshell. In the second section, we created our own port scanner with the help of Scapy and used it to gather more information about the potentially compromised systems.

After we discussed the areas of forensic algorithms, Windows and Unix systems, as well as the network layer, the following chapter will deal with virtualized systems and hypervisors that are becoming an important part of every company.

5
Using Python for Virtualization Forensics

Currently, virtualization is one of the most trending concepts of modern IT. For forensic analysis, it introduces new challenges as well as new techniques.

In this chapter, we will show how virtualization introduces the following:

- New attack vectors
- New chances of gathering evidence
- New targets for forensic analysis such as the virtualization layer
- New sources for forensic data

Considering virtualization as a new attack surface

Before we start with a forensic analysis, it is important to understand what to look for. With virtualization, there are new attack vectors and scenarios that are introduced. In the following sections, we will describe some of the scenarios and how to look for the corresponding evidence.

Virtualization as an additional layer of abstraction

Virtualization is the technique of emulating IT systems such as servers, workstations, networks, and storages. The component that is responsible for the emulation of virtual hardware is defined as **hypervisor**. The following figure depicts the two main types of system virtualization that are used today:

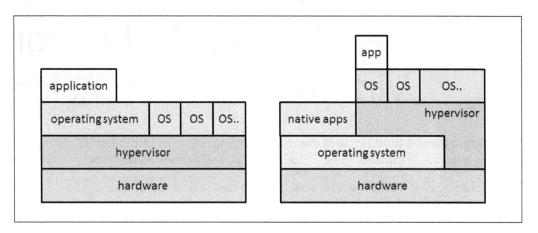

The architecture on the left-hand side is called **bare-metal hypervisor** architecture and is also known as a **Type 1** hypervisor. In this architecture, the hypervisor replaces the operating system and runs directly on the bare metal hardware. Examples of Type I hypervisors are VMware ESXi and Microsoft Hyper-V.

The right-hand side of the image depicts an architecture that is usually referred to as **desktop virtualization** or a **Type 2** hypervisor. In this architecture, there is a standard operating system that is running on the hardware, for example, a standard Windows 8 or Linux Desktop system. The hypervisor runs among other native applications directly on this operating system. Some functionality of the hypervisor may directly interact with the underlying hardware, for example, by providing special drivers. For Type 2 hypervisors, the operating system that is running directly on the hardware is called **host OS**, while the operating system running on a virtual machine is called **guest OS**. Examples of Type 2 hypervisor architectures are Oracle VirtualBox and VMware Workstation. These hypervisors can be installed just like any other application on an existing operating system.

 While Hyper-V seems like Type 2, it actually converts the host OS into just another guest OS during the installation and establishes a Type 1 architecture.

A common feature of almost all virtualization environments is the ability to create **snapshots**. A snapshot of a virtual system contains a frozen-in-time state of the system. All changes to the system that are happening after the snapshot creation can be undone by the hypervisor to roll back to the point in time when the snapshot was taken. Furthermore, most systems allow having multiple snapshots of a single system and rolling back and forward to arbitrary snapshots. Snapshots can be utilized as a source of forensic data, which we will demonstrate in the *Using virtualization as source of evidence* section.

For forensics, snapshots are to be treated like independent machines!

If a virtual system is subject to forensic analysis, always check whether this system is a virtual system and whether there are snapshots. If snapshots exist, the forensic analysis has to be repeated for every single snapshot as if this were an independent virtual machine. The rationale behind this requirement is that it is most likely unknown when the system was compromised, when the attacker tried to destroy evidence, and most importantly, what version of the machine was running during the attack.

Most virtualization environments consist of more than one hypervisor. To ease the management of multiple hypervisors and to enable additional features; for example, moving machines between hypervisors for fail over, load balancing, and save power; these environments provide a central management for all of hypervisors. In the case of VMware vSphere, this management component is called **vCenter Server**, as follows:

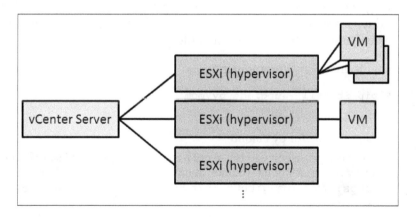

If **vCenter Server** is used, then all administrative tasks are supposed to be handled via this **vCenter Server** instance.

How does this new hypervisor layer influence attack scenarios and forensics?

The introduction of the new hypervisor layer also introduces a new layer that can be used to manipulate virtual systems without detection and adds another new layer that can be subject to the attacks. In the following sections, we will provide some sample scenarios for attacks that are committed through the hypervisor.

Creation of rogue machines

If an attacker can get access to the hypervisor, he may just create new virtual resources. These resources can act as a bridgehead in the network or just steal memory and compute resources from the environment. Therefore, it is crucial to extract the creation and disposal of virtual resources during a forensic analysis of the hypervisor environment.

Fortunately, every widespread virtualization environment offers APIs and language bindings to enumerate the virtual machines and other virtual resources of the environment. In this chapter, we chose to use VMware vSphere as the prominent example of a virtualization environment.

VMware vSphere is one of the most used virtualization environments for on-premise virtualization. Its basic structure consists of one central management instance called vCenter Server and one or multiple systems that are actually hosting the virtual environment (hypervisors), called **ESXi** servers. To programmatically control a vSphere environment with Python, pyVmomi is used. This Python SDK is available on Github at `https://github.com/vmware/pyvmomi`.

In the following, we will use `pyVmomi` to create a list of all virtual machines. It is recommended to run such inventory scan at regular intervals to compare the list of existing virtual assets with your local inventory database.

We recommend to install pyVmomi using `pip`:

```
user@lab:~$ pip install --upgrade pyVmomi
```

Sample code for pyVmomi

There is a project on GitHub about a community-provided sample code for pyVmomi. More information about these samples is available on `https://vmware.github.io/pyvmomi-community-samples/`.

Then, a script as shown in the following may be used to enumerate all systems of the vSphere environment:

```python
#!/usr/bin/env python

from pyVim import connect
from pyVmomi import vmodl
import sys

def print_vm_info(vm):
    """
    Print the information for the given virtual machine.
    If vm is a folder, recurse into that folder.
    """

    # check if this a folder...
    if hasattr(vm, 'childEntity'):
        vms = vm.childEntity
        for child in vms:
            print_vm_info(child)

    vm_info = vm.summary

    print 'Name:       ', vm_info.config.name
    print 'State:      ', vm_info.runtime.powerState
    print 'Path:       ', vm_info.config.vmPathName
    print 'Guest:      ', vm_info.config.guestFullName
    print 'UUID:       ', vm_info.config.instanceUuid
    print 'Bios UUID: ', vm_info.config.uuid
    print "----------\n"


if __name__ == '__main__':
    if len(sys.argv) < 5:
        print 'Usage: %s host user password port' % sys.argv[0]
        sys.exit(1)

    service = connect.SmartConnect(host=sys.argv[1],
                                   user=sys.argv[2],
                                   pwd=sys.argv[3],
                                   port=int(sys.argv[4]))

    # access the inventory
    content = service.RetrieveContent()
```

```
        children = content.rootFolder.childEntity

        # iterate over inventory
        for child in children:
            if hasattr(child, 'vmFolder'):
                dc = child
            else:
                # no folder containing virtual machines -> ignore
                continue

            vm_folder = dc.vmFolder
            vm_list = vm_folder.childEntity
            for vm in vm_list:
                print_vm_info(vm)
```

This script creates a connection to the vCenter Server platform. However, it can also be used to connect to a single ESXi hypervisor instance. This is possible because the API offered to the script is identical for both management variants.

 The API used by pyVmomi is the **vSphere Web Service API**. A detailed description is available in the vSphere Web Services SDK via https://www.vmware.com/support/developer/vc-sdk/.

The highlighted lines show that the script uses recursion to enumerate all virtual machines. This is necessary because in VMware vSphere, virtual machines can be put into nested groups.

Here is a sample call of this script with the output of a single virtual machine:

```
user@lab:~$ python enumerateVMs.py 192.168.167.26 'readonly' 'mypwd' 443
Name:       vCenterServer
State:       poweredOff
Path:        [datastore1] vCenterServer/vCenterServer.vmx
Guest:      Microsoft Windows Server 2012 (64-bit)
UUID:       522b96ec-7987-a974-98f1-ee8c4199dda4
Bios UUID: 564d8ec9-1b42-d235-a67c-d978c5107179
----------
```

The output lists the name of the virtual machine, its current state, the path of its configuration file, a hint for the guest operating system, and the unique IDs for the instance and the BIOS configuration. The path information is valuable, especially, because it shows where to find all the virtual machine's configuration and data file.

Cloning of systems

In the previous section, we used the API of the hypervisor to get the forensic data. In this section, we will look for traces of abuse of this API. Therefore, we will analyse the log information of the vSphere installation.

> **Collect log information on a central log system**
>
> In this section, we will assume that the log information is stored with the default settings of the vSphere installation. However, when setting up a system, we recommend to store the log information on a dedicated logging system. This makes it more difficult for an attacker to manipulate system logs as he requires access to not only his target system, but also to the central log collection system. Another advantage of many central log collection systems is the built-in log analysis function.

While a copy of all system logs is highly recommended for a forensically sound analysis, single events can also be reviewed using the event browser of VMware vSphere, as follows:

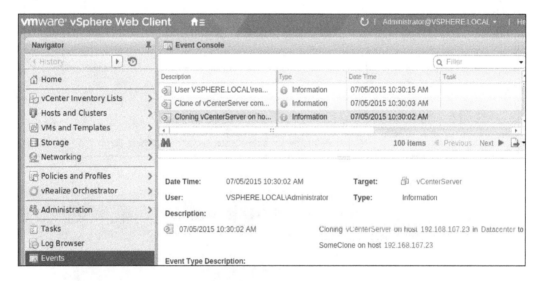

The vSphere environment offers collecting and storing all log files in an archive. Perform the following steps to get an archive of all the available log data:

- Use the Windows version of vSphere Web Client and log in to the **vCenter Server**.

- In the **Administration** menu, select **Export System Logs**.

- Select one or multiple vCenter Servers to export the logs, as shown in the following:

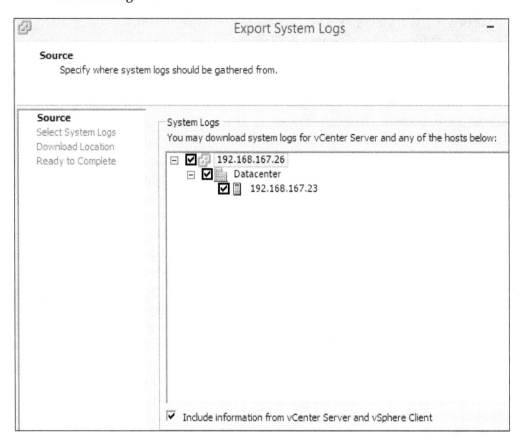

- When asked to **Select System Logs**, ensure that all log types are selected, as follows:

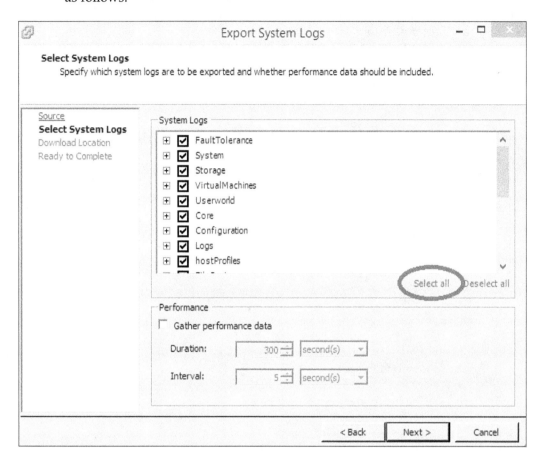

The log files are saved as compressed archives. One archive represents the log information of one system, that is, vCenter Server or ESXi host.

First, we will extract the collected log file using `tar` with a command as follows:

```
user@lab:~$ tar xfz 192.168.167.26-vcsupport-2015-07-05@11-21-54.tgz
```

The filename of this archive follows the format Host/IP—vcsupport (for vCenter Server)—timestamp. The directory in this archive follows the vc-Hostname-Timestamp naming scheme, for example, `vc-winserver-2015-07-05--02.19`. The timestamps of the archive name and the contained directory usually do not match. This can be caused due to the clock drift and the time required to transmit and compress the logs.

In the following, we will use the vCenter Server logs to reconstruct events indicating the cloning of virtual machines. In this example, we will use the redundancy of the logs and use the log data from one of the core services of vCenter Server: vpxd, that is, the core vCenter daemon:

```python
#!/usr/bin/env python

import gzip
import os
from os.path import join
import re
import sys


# used to map session IDs to users and source IPs
session2user_ip = {}

def _logopen(filename):
    """Helper to provide transparent decompressing of compressed logs,
        if indicated by the file name.
    """
    if re.match(r'.*\.gz', filename):
        return gzip.open(filename, 'r')

    return open(filename, 'r')

def collect_session_data(vpxlogdir):
    """Uses vpx performance logs to map the session ID to
        source user name and IP"""
    extract = re.compile(r'SessionStats/SessionPool/Session/
Id=\'([^\']+)\'/Username=\'([^\']+)\'/ClientIP=\'([^\']+)\'')

    logfiles = os.listdir(vpxlogdir)
    logfiles = filter(lambda x: 'vpxd-profiler-' in x, logfiles)
    for fname in logfiles:
        fpath = join(vpxlogdir, fname)
        f = _logopen(fpath)

        for line in f:
            m = extract.search(line)
            if m:
```

```
                    session2user_ip[m.group(1)] = (m.group(2), m.group(3))

        f.close()

def print_cloning_hints(basedir):
    """Print timestamp, user, and IP address for VM cloning without
        by reconstructing from vpxd logs instead of accessing
        the 'official' event logs"""
    vpxlogdir = join(basedir, 'ProgramData',
                              'vCenterServer',
                              'logs',
                              'vmware-vpx')
    collect_session_data(vpxlogdir)

    extract = re.compile(r'^([^ ]+).*BEGIN task-.*?vim\.
VirtualMachine\.clone -- ([0-9a-f-]+).*')

    logfiles = os.listdir(vpxlogdir)
    logfiles = filter(lambda x: re.match('vpxd-[0-9]+.log(.gz)?', x),
logfiles)
    logfiles.sort()

    for fname in logfiles:
        fpath = join(vpxlogdir, fname)
        f = _logopen(fpath)

        for line in f:
            m = extract.match(line)
            if m == None:
                continue

            timestamp = m.group(1)
            session = m.group(2)
            (user, ip) = session2user_ip.get(session,
('***UNKNOWN***', '***UNKNOWN***'))
            print 'Hint for cloning at %s by %s from %s' % (timestamp,
user, ip)

if __name__ == '__main__':
    if len(sys.argv) < 2:
        print 'Usage: %s vCenterLogDirectory' % sys.argv[0]
        sys.exit(1)

    print_cloning_hints(sys.argv[1])
```

First, this script reads the so-called performance log of vpxd. This log contains data about client sessions and we use it to extract a mapping from the unique session identifier to the client username and the IP address that the client is connecting from. In the second step, the main log of vpxd is searched for the start of tasks of vim. VirtualMachine.clone type, that is, the cloning of virtual machines on the server side. The session information is then looked up in the mapping that is harvested from the performance log to retrieve the data about possible cloning events, as follows:

```
user@lab:~$ python extractCloning.py vc-winserver-2015-07-05--02.19/
Hint for cloning at 2015-07-05T01:30:01.071-07:00 by VSPHERE.LOCAL\
Administrator from 192.168.167.26
```

In the example, the script revealed that the Administrator account was used to clone a virtual machine. This hint can be correlated with the event log of vCenter Server and it will show up there as well. If it does not, then this is a strong indicator of a compromised environment.

> Depending on your system environment, operations such as cloning and exporting virtual machines may be a part of daily operations. In that case, the previous script or its variants may be used to detect unusual users or source IPs that are performing these operations.

Similar searches and correlations can be used for other events of interest. Copying of files of the datastore or exporting virtual machines are promising candidates.

Searching for misuse of virtual resources

It is not just the motivated attacker that we are looking for. With virtualization, there is also the legitimate administrator of the virtual infrastructure who makes his life easier by bending some rules. Additionally, an attacker may use the power of virtualization to reshape the topology of the infrastructure according to his needs. In the following sections, we will show some scenarios and detection methods.

Detecting rogue network interfaces

Network virtualization allows operations to create almost arbitrary network infrastructures in a static, physical network. This capability is sometimes referred to as **Data center as a Service (DCaaS)**. DCaaS allows the customers to utilize a defined portion of a physical data center to define virtual data centers in software.

Due to malicious access to this capability or human error, the resulting network configuration may expose internal resources to the internet, bypass firewalls, or allow access to malicious services.

Therefore, we will show a simple way to programmatically get the network configuration of a vSphere environment using Python.

Visualize virtual networks

Most virtualization environments have built-in capabilities to visualize the virtual network setup. For example, VMware vSphere can create an image of the network topology. In a forensic analysis, this may serve as the starting point and support focusing the next step on the most promising assets.

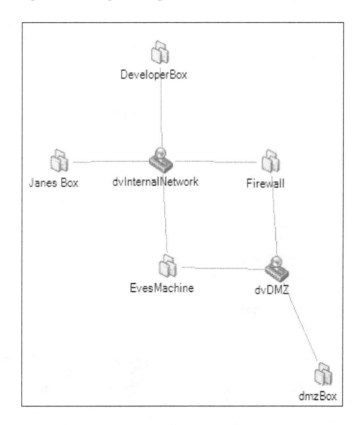

This image was generated with the Windows client software for VMware vCenter Server and it depicts our test setup. Obviously, **EvesMachine** is not connected properly, that is, it can bypass the **Firewall**.

The community sample scripts for `pyVmomi` already provide a script for iterating over all network interfaces, `https://github.com/vmware/pyvmomi-community-samples/blob/master/samples/getvnicinfo.py`, and displaying the connections of virtual machines. Therefore, we modified this script to display only those virtual machines that have multiple network connections, as follows:

```python
#!/usr/bin/env python

from pyVim import connect
from pyVmomi import vmodl
from pyVmomi import vim
import sys

def generate_portgroup_info(content):
    """Enumerates all hypervisors to get
       network infrastructure information"""
    host_view = content.viewManager.CreateContainerView(content.
rootFolder,
                                            [vim.HostSystem],
                                            True)
    hostlist = [host for host in host_view.view]
    host_view.Destroy()

    hostPgDict = {}
    for host in hostlist:
        pgs = host.config.network.portgroup
        hostPgDict[host] = pgs

    return (hostlist, hostPgDict)

def get_vms(content, min_nics=1):
    vm_view = content.viewManager.CreateContainerView(content.
rootFolder,
                                            [vim.VirtualMachine],
                                            True)
    vms = [vm for vm in vm_view.view]
    vm_view.Destroy()

    vm_with_nics = []
    for vm in vms:
        num_nics = 0
        for dev in vm.config.hardware.device:
            # ignore non-network devices
            if not isinstance(dev, vim.vm.device.VirtualEthernetCard):
```

```
            continue

        num_nics = num_nics + 1
        if num_nics >= min_nics:
            vm_with_nics.append(vm)
            break


    return vm_with_nics


def print_vm_info(vm, hosts, host2portgroup, content):
    print "\n=== %s ===" % vm.name

    for dev in vm.config.hardware.device:
        if not isinstance(dev, vim.vm.device.VirtualEthernetCard):
            continue

        dev_backing = dev.backing
        if hasattr(dev_backing, 'port'):
            # NIC is connected to distributed vSwitch
            portGroupKey = dev.backing.port.portgroupKey
            dvsUuid = dev.backing.port.switchUuid
            try:
                dvs = content.dvSwitchManager.QueryDvsByUuid(dvsUuid)
            except:
                portGroup = 'ERROR: DVS not found!'
                vlanId = 'N/A'
                vSwitch = 'N/A'
            else:
                pgObj = dvs.LookupDvPortGroup(portGroupKey)
                portGroup = pgObj.config.name
                vlObj = pgObj.config.defaultPortConfig.vlan
                if hasattr(vlObj, 'pvlanId'):
                    vlanId = str(pgObj.config.defaultPortConfig.vlan.
pvlanId)
                else:
                    vlanId = str(pgObj.config.defaultPortConfig.vlan.
vlanId)
                vSwitch = str(dvs.name)
        else:
            # NIC is connected to simple vSwitch
            portGroup = dev.backing.network.name
            vmHost = vm.runtime.host

            # look up the port group from the
```

```
                # matching host
                host_pos = hosts.index(vmHost)
                viewHost = hosts[host_pos]
                pgs = host2portgroup[viewHost]

                for p in pgs:
                    if portgroup in p.key:
                        vlanId = str(p.spec.vlanId)
                        vSwitch = str(p.spec.vswitchName)

            if portGroup is None:
                portGroup = 'N/A'

            print '%s -> %s @ %s -> %s (VLAN %s)' % (dev.deviceInfo.label,
                                                     dev.macAddress,
                                                     vSwitch,
                                                     portGroup,
                                                     vlanId)

def print_dual_homed_vms(service):
    """Lists all virtual machines with multiple
       NICs to different networks"""

    content = service.RetrieveContent()
    hosts, host2portgroup = generate_portgroup_info(content)
    vms = get_vms(content, min_nics=2)
    for vm in vms:
        print_vm_info(vm, hosts, host2portgroup, content)


if __name__ == '__main__':
    if len(sys.argv) < 5:
        print 'Usage: %s host user password port' % sys.argv[0]
        sys.exit(1)

    service = connect.SmartConnect(host=sys.argv[1],
                                   user=sys.argv[2],
                                   pwd=sys.argv[3],
                                   port=int(sys.argv[4]))
    print_dual_homed_vms(service)
```

First, this script iterates over all (hypervisor) hosts to collect information about the virtual switches that are present on each ESXi system. Then, it iterates over all virtual machines to collect those with more than one network card. Then the information about virtual network cards is combined with the information about virtual switches to derive the information about the connectivity.

Here is the sample output from our lab environment as depicted previously:

```
user@lab:~$ python listDualHomed.py 192.168.167.26 readonly 'mypwd' 443
=== EvesMachine ===
Network adapter 1 -> 00:50:56:ab:04:38 @ dvSwitch -> dvInternalNetwork
(VLAN 8)
Network adapter 2 -> 00:50:56:ab:23:50 @ dvSwitch -> dvDMZ (VLAN 0)

=== Firewall ===
Network adapter 1 -> 00:50:56:ab:12:e6 @ dvSwitch -> dvInternalNetwork
(VLAN 8)
Network adapter 2 -> 00:50:56:ab:4b:62 @ dvSwitch -> dvDMZ (VLAN 0)
```

Our script correctly identified the two systems, EvesMachine and Firewall, being simultaneously connected to different networks. In this particular case, both the systems can be used to connect VLAN 0 with VLAN 8 on the same virtual switch, dvSwitch.

Detecting direct hardware access

It may sound like an oxymoron, but most virtualization techniques allow direct hardware access. The legitimate reasons to allow virtual systems to directly access a piece of hardware without having to use the services of the hypervisor are as follows:

- **Special hardware supposed to be connected to a virtual machine**: Special hardware such as radio clocks for virtual time servers or dongles being part of a copy protection mechanism.

- **Temporary use of physical media on a virtual system**: Sometimes, this capability is used to access media from physical systems from a virtual environment, for example, to restore backups from a physical media to a virtual system. In general, the network attached storage systems should be preferred over attaching physical media to a virtual system.

- **Permanent use of drives of a hypervisor from a virtual machine**: This can be useful if the virtual system uses software that is provided on physical media and therefore, needs access to a real physical drive for installation and updates of the software. However, one should consider using downloaded versions or ISO images instead of granting direct access to the hardware of the hypervisor.

As you may guess, according to this list, direct hardware access is more the exception than the rule in a modern virtualized data center. Furthermore, direct access to the hypervisor hardware breaks one fundamental principle of virtualization.

> Direct hardware access bypasses the security mechanism of the virtualization environment, that is, all the virtual hardware is controlled by the hypervisor. Consequently, direct hardware access always poses the risk of manipulation of hypervisor resources, data leakage, and system instabilities.

The following are some examples of the directly attached hardware that are most likely malicious:

- Network devices (create network connections that are invisible to the hypervisor)
- Keyboard, mouse, and so on (create console access that are invisible to the hypervisor)
- Hypervisor disk partitions

The latter is especially dangerous. If a virtual machine manages to get the raw disk access to the hypervisor, it can manipulate the virtualization environment. The consequences include the complete control over the virtualization environment along with the access to all virtual machines, all virtual networks, the capability to create new rogue resources and reshape the overall network topology.

> For VMware vSphere, the direct hardware access is stored in the configuration of the virtual machines. Consequently, importing a virtual machine from an unknown or untrusted source (in the native format of vSphere) can create rogue hardware access.

The following script connects to a VMware vSphere instance and lists all virtual machines with direct hardware access:

```python
#!/usr/bin/env python

from pyVim import connect
from pyVmomi import vmodl
from pyVmomi import vim
import re
import sys


def get_vms(content):
```

```
        """Returns a list of all virtual machines."""
    vm_view = content.viewManager.CreateContainerView(content.
rootFolder,
                                            [vim.
VirtualMachine],
                                            True)

    vms = [vm for vm in vm_view.view]
    vm_view.Destroy()
    return vms


def print_vm_hardware_access(vm):
    findings = []

    for dev in vm.config.hardware.device:
        if isinstance(dev, vim.vm.device.VirtualUSB):
            findings.append('USB access to host device ' + dev.
backing.deviceName)
        elif isinstance(dev, vim.vm.device.VirtualSerialPort):
            findings.append('Serial port access')
        elif isinstance(dev, vim.vm.device.VirtualCdrom):
            if not dev.backing is None:
                if 'vmfs/devices/cdrom' in dev.backing.deviceName:
                    findings.append('Access to CD/DVD drive')
        elif isinstance(dev, vim.vm.device.VirtualDisk):
            if dev.backing is None or \
               dev.backing.fileName is None or \
               re.match(r'.*\.vmdk', dev.backing.fileName) is None:
                findings.append('Suspicious HDD configuration')

    if len(findings) > 0:
        print '=== %s hardware configuration findings ===' % vm.name
        for l in findings:
            print l
        print "\n"


def print_direct_hardware_access(content):
    vms = get_vms(content)
    for vm in vms:
        print_vm_hardware_access(vm)


if __name__ == '__main__':
    if len(sys.argv) < 5:
        print 'Usage: %s host user password port' % sys.argv[0]
```

```
        sys.exit(1)

    service = connect.SmartConnect(host=sys.argv[1],
                                    user=sys.argv[2],
                                    pwd=sys.argv[3],
                                    port=int(sys.argv[4]))

    # access the inventory
    content = service.RetrieveContent()
    print_direct_hardware_access(content)
```

This script is very eager, that is, it does not check whether the device is actually in a connected state or whether there is media accessible through the device. Nevertheless, an output similar to the following calls for deeper inspection:

```
user@lab:~$ python listHardwareAccess.py 192.168.167.26 readonly pwd 443
=== EvesMachine hardware configuration findings ===
Access to CD/DVD drive
Serial port access
USB access to host device path:2/0 version:2


=== DeveloperBox hardware configuration findings ===
Access to CD/DVD drive


=== dmzBox hardware configuration findings ===
Access to CD/DVD drive
```

EvesMachine appears to have direct access to a USB device attached to its hypervisor system. Moreover, there seems to be a direct link to the serial port of the hypervisor. Access to CD/DVD drive of the hypervisor should not be granted in general. However, for a lot of installations, people tend to use the optical drive of the hypervisor to install or update a software.

Extract hardware configuration from the VMX file

Using a script such as the previous one requires access to the virtual environment. Therefore, the main purpose of such scripts is to narrow the focus of the forensic investigation. For permanent evidence and record, the directory of the virtual machines should be copied from the datastore. There, the VMX file contains all VM specific configuration settings including the hardware access.

In this and the previous sections, virtualization is considered as an additional attack surface. In the following section, we will outline how virtualization techniques can actually support a forensic investigation.

Using virtualization as a source of evidence

Virtualization is not just dangerous and challenging when it comes to forensic investigations, there is also the potential to use virtualization as a tool for gathering forensic evidence. In the following sections, you will see various sources which can lead to the evidence.

Creating forensic copies of RAM content

Normally, creating a copy of a system's RAM contents requires access to the target system, a logon, installing the required tools, and copying away the RAM dump to an external media. All of these steps are intrusive, that is, changing the state of the system and being subject to detection by the attacker or his malware. Furthermore, an attacker with administrative privileges may hide portions of the system memory from the memory dumps, for example, by manipulating the memory allocation and protection algorithms.

To overcome the disadvantages of this method, the hypervisor layer can be utilized to get a complete, non-tampered copy of the memory of a virtual system. The following script can be used to create a snapshot including the RAM content of a virtual machine:

```python
#!/usr/bin/env python

from pyVim import connect
from pyVmomi import vim
from datetime import datetime
import sys

def make_snapshot(service, vmname):
    """Creates a snapshot of all virtual machines with the given
name"""

    snap_name = 'Memory_Snapshot'
```

```python
    snap_desc = 'Snapshot for investigation taken at ' + datetime.
now().isoformat()

    content = service.RetrieveContent()
    vm_view = content.viewManager.CreateContainerView(content.
rootFolder,
                                                    [vim.
VirtualMachine],
                                                         True)
    vms = [vm for vm in vm_view.view if vm.name==vmname]
    vm_view.Destroy()

    for vm in vms:
        print 'Taking snapshot from VM UUID=%s' % vm.summary.config.
uuid
        vm.CreateSnapshot_Task(name = snap_name,
                               description = snap_desc,
                               memory = True,
                               quiesce=False)
        print "Done.\n"


if __name__ == '__main__':
    if len(sys.argv) < 6:
        print 'Usage: %s host user password port vmname' % sys.argv[0]
        sys.exit(1)

    service = connect.SmartConnect(host=sys.argv[1],
                                   user=sys.argv[2],
                                   pwd=sys.argv[3],
                                   port=int(sys.argv[4]))



    make_snapshot(service, sys.argv[5])
```

This script searches for virtual machines with the specified name and creates a snapshot. The highlighted parameter causes vSphere to write the RAM contents of the virtual machine to the datastore along with the other snapshot data files.

These RAM dumps reside in the directory of the virtual machine. The enumeration script in this chapter shows the path to this directory. Additionally, the vSphere Client allows browsing and downloading the datastore of the virtual machine.

The RAM contents are stored in a file with the .vmem extension, for example, EvesMachine-Snapshot2.vmem.

Using snapshots as disk images

For physical systems, creating a forensic disk image usually incorporates taking the system offline, shutting it down, removing the hard drive, and copying it. Obviously, the system is not operational during this procedure and as a consequence, business owners are very reluctant in granting these downtimes due to a vague suspicion of a possible compromise.

On the other hand, the creation of a snapshot of a virtual machine results in basically no downtime but the result is a forensically sound disk image of the virtual asset.

Always check whether a system is virtual!

As the creation of forensic data is much easier for virtual systems than for physical systems, one of the very first steps in a forensic investigation should be checking whether the target system is virtual.

The creation of the snapshot is identical to the script in the previous section. For VMware vSphere 5, all the files have to be copied from the datastore directory of the hypervisor to get a complete dump of the hard drives. If the virtual system is still running, some files may not get copied as the hypervisor will not allow read access while these files are in use. Typically, this is not a problem as these files are only needed by the snapshot, that is, all the changes since the creation of the snapshot are stored in special snapshot files.

In VMware vSphere 6, the snapshot mechanism has been changed. Instead of writing disk changes in the snapshot files, the changes made after snapshot creation are directly written to the files that represent the virtual hard drives. The snapshot files are used to preserve the original contents of the disk drives (copy-on-write behavior).

Therefore, the files that are to be copied from a VMware vSphere 6 environment will contain all entries of the directory of the virtual machine.

For the forensic analysis, the captured disk images can be connected to a virtual forensic workstation. There, these images can be treated like any other physical hard drive. Of course, the original copies must remain intact in order to provide forensic soundness.

Capturing network traffic

The virtualization environment not only represents virtual machines and **Network Interfaces Card** (**NIC**), but also the virtual network devices that are needed to interconnect these systems. This combination can be used to collect all the network traffic of a virtual network by adding a monitoring port to the virtual switch and connecting a system to it, which can capture all the network traffic.

 If a virtual system in VMware vSphere is allowed to switch a NIC into a promiscuous mode, then this will automatically turn the corresponding switch port into the monitoring mode.

Furthermore, the enterprise editions of VMware vSphere provide an advanced version of a virtual switch called **vSphere Distributed Switch** (**VDS**). This switch can act more like a physical switch and provide mirroring of selected ports to a defined port for the traffic analysis. In addition, this switch is also capable of providing NetFlow logs to a defined port.

For the standard virtual switch, the following steps are required in order to monitor the network traffic:

* Create a new port group on this switch to monitor. While this is not strictly required, it is highly recommended. Without a dedicated port group to monitor, all virtual systems on the switch would be allowed to monitor all the traffic of the switch.

* Modify the **Security** settings of this port group and change the **Promiscuous mode** to **Accept**.

* Configure the network card of the virtual capture system to the new port group. This system can now capture all the network traffic of this switch.

The exact steps may differ between virtual switch types and their versions. Nevertheless, the core message is that virtualization environments can ease this task of network traffic capturing. Moreover, physical and virtual switches do have different behaviors, for example, they can react to configuration changes of the connected network cards.

In the next chapter, we will see how to generate and analyze this captured network traffic.

Summary

In this chapter, we outlined how virtualization changes the landscape not just for IT operations, but also for the attacker and forensic specialist. Systems can be created, reshaped, and copied for good and bad reasons.

We provided examples of how to detect possibly malicious behavior or configuration on the vSphere virtualization environment. Moreover, we demonstrated how virtualization can be beneficial in getting untampered RAM dumps from the systems that should be analyzed. In the next chapter, you will see examples on how to analyze these RAM dumps.

With this knowledge, you are now prepared to analyze and utilize virtual environments in your forensic analyses.

6
Using Python for Mobile Forensics

While forensic analysis of standard computer hardware — such as hard disks — has developed into a stable discipline with a lot of reference work such as the book *File System Forensic Analysis*, by *Brian Carrier*, *Addison-Wesley Professional* and our previous chapters, there is still much debate on the techniques to analyze non-standard hardware or transient evidence. Despite their increasing role in digital investigations, smartphones are still to be considered non-standard because of their heterogeneity. In all the investigations, it is necessary to follow the basic forensic principles. The two main principles of forensic investigations are as follows:

- Great care must be taken so that the evidence is manipulated or changed as little as possible.

- The course of a digital investigation must be understandable and open to scrutiny. At best, the results of the investigation must be reproducible by independent investigators.

The first principle, especially, is a challenge in in case of smartphones as most of them employ specific operating systems and hardware protection methods that prevent unrestricted access to the data on the system.

The preservation of data from hard disks is, in most cases, a simple and well-known procedure. An investigator removes the hard disk from the computer or notebook, connects it to his workstation with the help of a write blocker (for example, Tableau TK35) and starts analyzing it with well-known and certified software solutions. When comparing this to the smartphone world, it becomes clear that there is no such procedure. Nearly every smartphone has its own way to build its storage in and ongoing with this, for each smartphone, the investigator needs their own way to get the dump of the storage. While it is very hard to get the data from a smartphone, one can get much more data with reference to the diversity of the data. Smartphones store, besides the usual data (for example, pictures and documents), the data such as GPS coordinates and the position of a mobile cell that the smartphone was connected to before it was switched off.

Considering the resulting opportunities, it turns out that it is worth the extra expense for an investigator.

In this chapter, we will cover the following topics:

- The investigative model from *Eoghan Casey* adopted by smartphones
- The analysis of Android smartphones (manual as well as automated through **Android Data Extractor Lite (ADEL)**)
- The analysis of iOS smartphones

The investigative model for smartphones

The **Investigative Process Model** by *Eoghan Casey*, which is also known as the **Staircase Model**, provides a practical and methodical step-by-step guide to conduct an effective digital investigation. This model is depicted as a sequence of ascending stairs that begin at the incident alert or accusation and end at the testimony. The steps are meant to be as generic as possible. This model tries to merge police duties and tasks of forensic experts. The following points explain each step of the Investigative Process Model and the difference between dealing with smartphones and computers:

- **Incident Alerts or Accusation**: The accusation is the start signal for the whole process. In this phase, the sources are evaluated and detailed inquiries are requested.

- **Assessment of worth**: In the scope of the assessment of worth, the interest of prosecution is compared to the costs that would be incurred to prosecute the criminal action. For companies, this often results in a decision against prosecution (for smaller incidents, at least). The advantages of a prosecution lie in the possible compensation, improvement of one's own security as well as certain effect of deterrence. The disadvantages of a prosecution are the need of resources, possible downtime during which the investigated systems cannot be used productively, and most of the time a negative public scatter effect.

- **Incident or crime scene protocols**: In classic criminalistics, it is often demanded that the crime scene is spaciously closed. *Eoghan Casey* expresses this as the following:

  > *"Freeze" the evidence in place and provide "ground truth for all activities that follow"*.

  For different kinds of digital traces, it has to be checked on an individual basis how the process of freezing is exactly defined. Altogether, it holds true that the risk of changing traces has to be minimized. For smartphones, this means that they have to be put in a Faraday bag that is connected to an external power supply.

- **Identification or seizure**: During a traditional impoundment, all objects and subjects that could act as evidence are picked up. Here, it is important that no changes are made to the evidence. In addition, the environment of evidence might be of great relevance. Simultaneous to the impoundment, the chain of custody starts. A recommended paper about the impoundment is the brochure, *Electronic Crime Scene Investigation: A Guide to First Responders*, published by *The United States Department of Justice*. This brochure provides accurate and detailed tips for nontechnical staff. Another good source is the document, *Searching and Seizing Computers and Obtaining Electronic Evidence in Criminal Investigations*, also published by *The United States Department of Justice*.

- **Preservation**: When securing the evidence, it has to be ensured that these are not modified. This is why all the evidence is documented, photographed, sealed, and afterwards locked away. In the case of digital evidence, this means that copies of evidence are created first; further investigation is done only on the copies. To prove the authenticity of copies of evidence, cryptographic hash functions are used. Most often, this is the hardest part in mobile phone forensics due to the fact that creating one-to-one copies is not possible for some type of phones. We will show, in the following section, how to create backups that can be used during the investigation.

- **Recovery**: *Eoghan Casey* describes the retrieval as *throwing out a large net*. In particular, this phase includes the retrieval of evidence that has been deleted, hidden, masked, or made inaccessible in any other way. It is recommended that you make use of synergies with other evidence. For example, it is reasonable to test whether a note with passwords has been found at the crime scene in case the encrypted data needs to be read.

- **Harvesting**: During the analysis of evidence, a well-structured organization with a huge amount of data that is needed. For this reason, one should first investigate metadata instead of the real data. For example, the data can be grouped according to the file type or access time. This directly leads to the next phase, the reduction.

- **Reduction**: The task of reduction lies in eliminating irrelevant data. One can use metadata for this reason, too. For example, data can be reduced according to the data type. A suitable scenario would be to reduce all the data to image data, only if the accusation allows for this proceeding. The result of this phase is— according to *Eoghan Casey*:

  > *The smallest set of digital information that has the highest potential for containing data of probative value.*

  This means finding the smallest amount of data that has the highest probability of being relevant and evidential. In this context, hash databases of known files, such as The **National Software Reference Library** (**NIST**), are helpful to exclude already known files (we have described using this library in *Chapter 2, Forensic Algorithms*).

- **Organization and search**: The aspects of organization are structuring and enabling data for scanning. Therefore, indices and overviews are often created or their type sorts the files in meaningful directories. This simplifies the referencing of the data in the following steps.

- **Analysis**: This phase includes the detailed analysis regarding the file content. Among others, connections between data and persons have to be drawn in order to determine the responsible person. Moreover, the evaluation of the content and context is made according to the means, motivation, and opportunity. In this step, experiments are helpful to determine undocumented behavior and develop new methods. All results need to be tested and should be testable with scientific methodology.

- **Reporting**: The report is not only to present results but also demonstrate how one has arrived to the stated results. For this, all considered rules and standards should be documented. In addition, all drawn conclusions need to be justified and alternative explanation models need to be discussed.

- **Persuasion and Testimony**: Finally, it comes to the testimony of an authority on the subject at court. The most important aspect is the trustworthiness of the authority. A technology averse audience or difficult analogies, for example from the defense lawyer, can be problematic.

By looking at the previously described process, one can see only little changes when dealing with smartphones unlike other types of evidence. However, it is very important for an investigator to understand at what steps he has to take special care.

Android

The first mobile operating system that we will examine with the help of Python is Android. In the first subsection, we will demonstrate how to manually examine the smartphone, followed by an automatic approach using ADEL. Last but not least, we will demonstrate how to merge data from the analysis to create movement profiles.

Manual Examination

The first step is getting root access to the smartphone. This is required to circumvent internal system protections and get access to all data. Getting root access is different for most of the phones and strongly dependent on the OS version. The best way is creating your own **recovery image** and booting the phone through the built-in recovery mode.

After getting the root access, the next step is trying to get the screen lock in plain text as this *secret* is often used for different protections (for example, the screen lock can be used as an application password for an app on the phone). Breaking the screen lock for a PIN or password can be done with the following script:

```
import os, sys, subprocess, binascii, struct
import sqlite3 as lite

def get_sha1hash(backup_dir):

    # dumping the password/pin from the device
    print "Dumping PIN/Password hash ..."
    password = subprocess.Popen(['adb', 'pull', '/data/system/
password.key', backup_dir],
        stdout=subprocess.PIPE, stdin=subprocess.PIPE,
stderr=subprocess.PIPE)
    password.wait()

    # cutting the HASH within password.key
```

```
        sha1hash = open(backup_dir + '/password.key', 'r').readline()[:40]
        print "HASH: \033[0;32m" + sha1hash + "\033[m"

        return sha1hash

def get_salt(backup_dir):

        # dumping the system DB containing the SALT
        print "Dumping locksettings.db ..."
        saltdb = subprocess.Popen(['adb', 'pull', '/data/system/
locksettings.db', backup_dir],
                stdout=subprocess.PIPE, stdin=subprocess.PIPE,
stderr=subprocess.PIPE)
        saltdb.wait()
        saltdb2 = subprocess.Popen(['adb', 'pull', '/data/system/
locksettings.db-wal', backup_dir],
                stdout=subprocess.PIPE, stdin=subprocess.PIPE,
stderr=subprocess.PIPE)
        saltdb2.wait()
        saltdb3 = subprocess.Popen(['adb', 'pull', '/data/system/
locksettings.db-shm', backup_dir],
                stdout=subprocess.PIPE, stdin=subprocess.PIPE,
stderr=subprocess.PIPE)
        saltdb3.wait()

        # extract the SALT
        con = lite.connect(backup_dir + '/locksettings.db')
        cur = con.cursor()
        cur.execute("SELECT value FROM locksettings WHERE
name='lockscreen.password_salt'")
        salt = cur.fetchone()[0]
        con.close()

        # convert SALT to Hex
        returnedsalt =  binascii.hexlify(struct.pack('>q', int(salt) ))
        print "SALT: \033[0;32m" + returnedsalt + "\033[m"

        return returnedsalt


def write_crack(salt, sha1hash, backup_dir):

        crack = open(backup_dir + '/crack.hash', 'a+')

        # write HASH and SALT to cracking file
```

```
    hash_salt = sha1hash + ':' + salt
    crack.write(hash_salt)
    crack.close()


if __name__ == '__main__':

    # check if device is connected and adb is running as root
    if subprocess.Popen(['adb', 'get-state'], stdout=subprocess.PIPE).
communicate(0)[0].split("\n")[0] == "unknown":
        print "no device connected - exiting..."
        sys.exit(2)

    # starting to create the output directory and the crack file used
for hashcat
    backup_dir = sys.argv[1]

    try:
        os.stat(backup_dir)
    except:
        os.mkdir(backup_dir)

    sha1hash = get_sha1hash(backup_dir)
    salt = get_salt(backup_dir)
    write_crack(salt, sha1hash, backup_dir)
```

This script generates a file called `crack.hash` that can be used to feed **hashcat** to brute force the screen lock. If the smartphone owner has used a 4-digit PIN, the command to execute hashcat is as follows:

```
user@lab:~$ ./hashcat -a 3 -m 110 out/crack.hash -1 ?d ?1?1?1?1
Initializing hashcat v0.50 with 4 threads and 32mb segment-size...

Added hashes from file crack.hash: 1 (1 salts)
Activating quick-digest mode for single-hash with salt

c87226fed37977772be870d722c449f915844922:256c05b54b73308b:0420

All hashes have been recovered

Input.Mode: Mask (?1?1?1?1) [4]
Index.....: 0/1 (segment), 10000 (words), 0 (bytes)
```

```
Recovered.: 1/1 hashes, 1/1 salts
Speed/sec.: - plains, 7.71k words
Progress..: 7744/10000 (77.44%)
Running...: 00:00:00:01
Estimated.: --:--:--:--


Started: Sat Jul 20 17:14:52 2015
Stopped: Sat Jul 20 17:14:53 2015
```

By looking at the marked line in the output, you can see the sha256 hash followed by the salt and the brute forced PIN that is used to unlock the screen.

If the smartphone user has used a gesture to unlock the smartphone, you can use a pre-generated rainbow table and the following script:

```python
import hashlib, sqlite3, array, datetime
from binascii import hexlify

SQLITE_DB = "GestureRainbowTable.db"

def crack(backup_dir):

    # dumping the system file containing the hash
    print "Dumping gesture.key ..."

    saltdb = subprocess.Popen(['adb', 'pull', '/data/system/gesture.
key', backup_dir],
        stdout=subprocess.PIPE, stdin=subprocess.PIPE,
stderr=subprocess.PIPE)

    gesturehash = open(backup_dir + "/gesture.key", "rb").readline()
    lookuphash = hexlify(gesturehash).decode()
    print "HASH: \033[0;32m" + lookuphash + "\033[m"

    conn = sqlite3.connect(SQLITE_DB)
    cur = conn.cursor()
    cur.execute("SELECT pattern FROM RainbowTable WHERE hash = ?",
(lookuphash,))
    gesture = cur.fetchone()[0]

    return gesture

if __name__ == '__main__':

    # check if device is connected and adb is running as root
```

```
    if subprocess.Popen(['adb', 'get-state'], stdout=subprocess.PIPE).
communicate(0)[0].split("\n")[0] == "unknown":
        print "no device connected - exiting..."
        sys.exit(2)


    # starting to create the output directory and the crack file used
for hashcat
    backup_dir = sys.argv[1]

    try:
        os.stat(backup_dir)
    except:
        os.mkdir(backup_dir)

    gesture = crack(backup_dir)

    print "screenlock gesture: \033[0;32m" + gesture + "\033[m""
```

The next thing that could be very important when looking for potentially infected devices is a list of installed apps and their hashes to check them against **AndroTotal** or **Mobile-Sandbox**. This can be done with the following script:

```
import os, sys, subprocess, hashlib


def get_apps():

    # dumping the list of installed apps from the device
    print "Dumping apps meta data ..."

    meta = subprocess.Popen(['adb', 'shell', 'ls', '-l', '/data/app'],
        stdout=subprocess.PIPE, stdin=subprocess.PIPE,
stderr=subprocess.PIPE)
    meta.wait()

    apps = []
    while True:
        line = meta.stdout.readline()
        if line != '':
            name = line.split(' ')[-1].rstrip()
            date = line.split(' ')[-3]
            time = line.split(' ')[-2]
            if name.split('.')[-1] == 'apk':
                app = [name, date, time]
            else:
```

```
                        continue
                else:
                    break
                apps.append(app)

        return apps


    def dump_apps(apps, backup_dir):

        # dumping the apps from the device
        print "Dumping the apps ..."

        for app in apps:
            app = app[0]
            subprocess.Popen(['adb', 'pull', '/data/app/' + app, backup_
    dir],
                    stdout=subprocess.PIPE, stdin=subprocess.PIPE,
    stderr=subprocess.PIPE)


    def get_hashes(apps, backup_dir):

        # calculating the hashes
        print "Calculating the sha256 hashes ..."

        meta = []
        for app in apps:
            sha256 = hashlib.sha256(open(backup_dir + '/' + app[0], 'rb').
    read()).hexdigest()
            app.append(sha256)
            meta.append(app)

        return meta


    if __name__ == '__main__':

        # check if device is connected and adb is running as root
        if subprocess.Popen(['adb', 'get-state'], stdout=subprocess.PIPE).
    communicate(0)[0].split("\n")[0] == "unknown":
            print "no device connected - exiting..."
            sys.exit(2)

        # starting to create the output directory
```

```
backup_dir = sys.argv[1]

try:
    os.stat(backup_dir)
except:
    os.mkdir(backup_dir)

apps = get_apps()
dump_apps(apps, backup_dir)
meta = get_hashes(apps, backup_dir)

# printing the list of installed apps
print 'Installed apps:'
for app in meta:
    print "\033[0;32m" + ' '.join(app) + "\033[m"
```

After executing the preceding printed script, you get the following output including important metadata:

```
user@lab:~$ ./get_installed_apps.py out


Dumping apps meta data ...
Dumping the apps ...
Calculating the sha256 hashes ...


Installed apps:
com.android.SSLTrustKiller-1.apk 2015-05-18 17:11
52b4d6a1888a6514b62f6607cebf8c2c2aa4e4857319ec67b24be601db5243fb

com.android.chrome-2.apk 2015-06-16 20:50
191cd720626df38eaedf3301826e72330493cdeb8c45da4e309939cfe5633d61

com.android.vending-1.apk 2015-07-25 12:05
7be9f8f99e8c1a6c3be1edb01d84aba14619e3c67c14856755523413ba8e2d98

com.google.android.GoogleCamera-2.apk 2015-06-16 20:49
6936f3c17948c767550c206ff0ae0f44f1f4da0fcb85125da722e0c709787894

com.google.android.apps.authenticator2-1.apk 2015-06-05 10:14
11bcfcf1c853b1eb567c9453507c3413b09a1d70fd3085013f4a091719560ab6

...
```

With the help of this information, you can check the apps against online services to know whether they are safe to use or potentially malicious. If you don't want to submit them, then you can use the apk_analyzer.py script in combination with **Androguard** to perform a quick analysis that often can reveal important information.

After getting a list of all installed apps and checking them for malicious behavior, it can also be really helpful to get information about all partitions and mount points of the device. This can be achieved with the following script:

```python
import sys, subprocess


def get_partition_info():

    # dumping the list of installed apps from the device
    print "Dumping partition information ..."

    partitions = subprocess.Popen(['adb', 'shell', 'mount'],
        stdout=subprocess.PIPE, stdin=subprocess.PIPE,
stderr=subprocess.PIPE)
    partitions.wait()

    while True:
        line = partitions.stdout.readline().rstrip()
        if line != '':
            print "\033[0;32m" + line + "\033[m"
        else:
            break


if __name__ == '__main__':

    # check if device is connected and adb is running as root
    if subprocess.Popen(['adb', 'get-state'], stdout=subprocess.PIPE).
communicate(0)[0].split("\n")[0] == "unknown":
        print "no device connected - exiting..."
        sys.exit(2)

    get_partition_info()
```

The output of a rooted phone could look like this:

```
user@lab:~$ ./get_partitions.py

Dumping partition information ...
rootfs / rootfs rw,relatime 0 0
tmpfs /dev tmpfs rw,seclabel,nosuid,relatime,mode=755 0 0
devpts /dev/pts devpts rw,seclabel,relatime,mode=600 0 0
proc /proc proc rw,relatime 0 0
sysfs /sys sysfs rw,seclabel,relatime 0 0
selinuxfs /sys/fs/selinux selinuxfs rw,relatime 0 0
debugfs /sys/kernel/debug debugfs rw,relatime 0 0
none /acct cgroup rw,relatime,cpuacct 0 0
none /sys/fs/cgroup tmpfs rw,seclabel,relatime,mode=750,gid=1000 0 0
tmpfs /mnt/asec tmpfs rw,seclabel,relatime,mode=755,gid=1000 0 0
tmpfs /mnt/obb tmpfs rw,seclabel,relatime,mode=755,gid=1000 0 0
none /dev/cpuctl cgroup rw,relatime,cpu 0 0
/dev/block/platform/msm_sdcc.1/by-name/system /system ext4 ro,seclabel,re
latime,data=ordered 0 0
/dev/block/platform/msm_sdcc.1/by-name/userdata /data ext4 rw
,seclabel,nosuid,nodev,noatime,nomblk_io_submit,noauto_da_
alloc,errors=panic,data=ordered 0 0
/dev/block/platform/msm_sdcc.1/by-name/cache /cache ext4 rw
,seclabel,nosuid,nodev,noatime,nomblk_io_submit,noauto_da_
alloc,errors=panic,data=ordered 0 0
/dev/block/platform/msm_sdcc.1/by-name/persist /persist ext4 rw,seclabel,
nosuid,nodev,relatime,nomblk_io_submit,nodelalloc,errors=panic,data=order
ed 0 0
/dev/block/platform/msm_sdcc.1/by-name/modem /firmware vfat ro,relatime,u
id=1000,gid=1000,fmask=0337,dmask=0227,codepage=cp437,iocharset=iso8859-
1,shortname=lower,errors=remount-ro 0 0
/dev/fuse /mnt/shell/emulated fuse rw,nosuid,nodev,relatime,user_
id=1023,group_id=1023,default_permissions,allow_other 0 0
```

At the end of this section, we will show you how to gather more details about the usage of the android-based smartphone. In the following example, we will use the contacts database that also stores the phone call history. This example can easily be adopted to get calendar entries or content from any other database of an app that is installed on the device:

```python
import os, sys, subprocess
import sqlite3 as lite
from prettytable import from_db_cursor


def dump_database(backup_dir):

    # dumping the password/pin from the device
    print "Dumping contacts database ..."

    contactsDB = subprocess.Popen(['adb', 'pull', '/data/data/com.
android.providers.contacts/databases/contacts2.db',
        backup_dir], stdout=subprocess.PIPE, stdin=subprocess.PIPE,
stderr=subprocess.PIPE)
    contactsDB.wait()


def get_content(backup_dir):

    # getting the content from the contacts database
    con = lite.connect(backup_dir + '/contacts2.db')
    cur = con.cursor()
    cur.execute("SELECT contacts._id AS _id,contacts.custom_ringtone
AS custom_ringtone, name_raw_contact.display_name_source AS display_
name_source, name_raw_contact.display_name AS display_name, name_
raw_contact.display_name_alt AS display_name_alt, name_raw_contact.
phonetic_name AS phonetic_name, name_raw_contact.phonetic_name_style
AS phonetic_name_style, name_raw_contact.sort_key AS sort_key, name_
raw_contact.phonebook_label AS phonebook_label, name_raw_contact.
phonebook_bucket AS phonebook_bucket, name_raw_contact.sort_key_alt
AS sort_key_alt, name_raw_contact.phonebook_label_alt AS phonebook_
label_alt, name_raw_contact.phonebook_bucket_alt AS phonebook_
bucket_alt, has_phone_number, name_raw_contact_id, lookup, photo_id,
photo_file_id, CAST(EXISTS (SELECT _id FROM visible_contacts WHERE
contacts._id=visible_contacts._id) AS INTEGER) AS in_visible_group,
status_update_id, contacts.contact_last_updated_timestamp, contacts.
last_time_contacted AS last_time_contacted, contacts.send_to_voicemail
AS send_to_voicemail, contacts.starred AS starred, contacts.pinned
AS pinned, contacts.times_contacted AS times_contacted, (CASE WHEN
photo_file_id IS NULL THEN (CASE WHEN photo_id IS NULL OR photo_id=0
THEN NULL ELSE 'content://com.android.contacts/contacts/'||contacts._
```

```
id|| '/photo' END) ELSE 'content://com.android.contacts/display_
photo/'||photo_file_id END) AS photo_uri, (CASE WHEN photo_id IS
NULL OR photo_id=0 THEN NULL ELSE 'content://com.android.contacts/
contacts/'||contacts._id|| '/photo' END) AS photo_thumb_uri, 0 AS
is_user_profile FROM contacts JOIN raw_contacts AS name_raw_contact
ON(name_raw_contact_id=name_raw_contact._id)")
    pt = from_db_cursor(cur)
    con.close()


    print pt


if __name__ == '__main__':

    # check if device is connected and adb is running as root
    if subprocess.Popen(['adb', 'get-state'], stdout=subprocess.PIPE).
communicate(0)[0].split("\n")[0] == "unknown":
        print "no device connected - exiting..."
        sys.exit(2)

    # starting to create the output directory
    backup_dir = sys.argv[1]

    try:
        os.stat(backup_dir)
    except:
        os.mkdir(backup_dir)

    dump_database(backup_dir)
    get_content(backup_dir)
```

After you have seen how to manually perform an analysis of a smartphone, we will show you, in the upcoming section, how to perform the same actions that are automated with the help of ADEL.

Automated Examination with the help of ADEL

We have developed a tool named ADEL. It was initially developed for versions 2.x of Android but was updated to fit the needs of analysing Android 4.x smartphones. This tool is able to automatically dump the selected SQLite database files from Android devices and extract the contents that are stored in the dumped files. As a further option, ADEL is able to analyse databases that were dumped manually beforehand. This option was implemented to support smartphones where ADEL is not able to access the filesystem of the device due to security features like locked bootloaders. In the following sections, we describe the main tasks of ADEL and what steps the tool actually performs.

Idea behind the system

During the development of ADEL, we primarily took into account the following design guidelines:

- **Forensic principles**: ADEL is intended to treat data in a forensically correct way. This goal is achieved by the fact that activities are not conducted directly on the phone but on a copy of the databases. This procedure assures that the data is not modified either by the users of ADEL or by a compromised operating system. In order to providing the proof of the forensic correctness of ADEL, hash values are calculated before and after each analysis to guarantee that the dumped data was not modified during the analysis.

- **Extendibility**: ADEL has been modularly built and contains two separate modules: the analysis and the report module. Predefined interfaces exist between these modules and both of them can be easily amended with the help of additional functions. The modular structure allows you to dump and analyse further databases of smartphones without great effort and facilitates updates of the system in the future.

- **Usability**: The use of ADEL is intended to be as simple as possible to allow its use by both, qualified persons and non-experts. At best, the analysis of the mobile phone is conducted in an autonomous way so that the user does not receive any notification of internal processes. Moreover, the report module creates a detailed report in a readable form including all the decoded data. During the execution, ADEL optionally writes an extensive log file where all the important steps that were executed are traced.

Implementation and system workflow

A flow chart showing the structure of ADEL is depicted in the following figure:

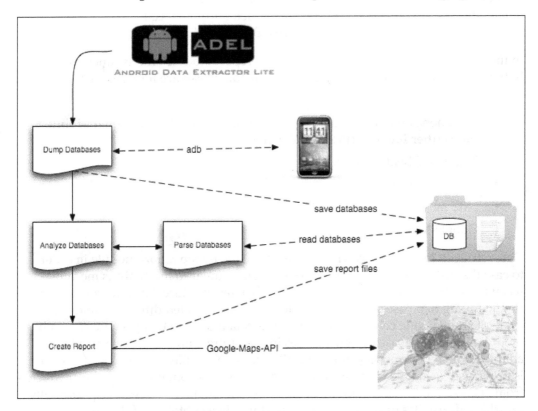

ADEL makes use of **Android Software Development Kit (Android SDK)** to dump database files in the investigator's machine. To extract contents that are contained in a SQLite database file, ADEL parses the low-level data structures. After having opened the database file that is to be parsed in the read-only mode, ADEL reads the database header (the first 100 bytes of the file) and extracts the values for each of the header fields. Not all, but some of the values in header fields are necessary in order to parse the rest of the database file. An important value is the size of the pages in the database file, which is required for parsing the B-tree structures (pagewise). After having read the database header fields, ADEL parses the B-tree that contains the sqlite_master table for which the first page of the database is always the root page. The SQL CREATE statement and the page number of the B-tree root page are extracted for each of the database tables. Additionally, the SQL CREATE statement is further analyzed to extract the name and data type of each column of the corresponding table.

Finally, the complete B-tree structure is parsed for each table, beginning at the B-tree root page, which was extracted from the `sqlite_master` table. By following the pointers of all of the interior pages, you can identify every leaf page of the B-tree. Finally the row contents of each table are extracted from the cells that are found in any leaf page that belongs to the same table B-tree.

In the following sections, we will address the report module and its functionalities. In the current development state, the following databases are forensically treated and parsed:

- Telephone and SIM-card information (for example **International Mobile Subscriber Identity** (**IMSI**) and serial number)
- Telephone book and call lists
- Calendar entries
- SMS messages
- Google-Maps

Data retrieved in this way is written to an XML file by the report module in order to ease the further use and depiction of the data. Similar to the analysis module, it can be easily updated regarding possible changes in future Android versions or in underlying database schemes. Therefore, we have created different tuple — for example, [table, row, column] — to define the data that is exchanged between both modules. If the database design changes in the future, only the tuple has to be adapted. The report module automatically creates XML files for each data type that is previously listed. In addition, a report is created that contains all the data extracted from analyzed databases. With the help of an XSL file the report will be graphically refurbished. All files created by ADEL are stored in a subfolder of the current project.

To get access to the necessary databases and system folders on the smartphone, ADEL needs root access on the device.

Working with ADEL

After we have described what ADEL is and how it works, we will now go to the practical part of this section and start using it. You can download ADEL from the following URL: `https://mspreitz.github.io/ADEL`

All you need to do is check whether the device in question is already included in the configuration profile of ADEL that is located in /xml/phone_config.xml. If the device is missing, there are two options on how to proceed:

1. Choose a different device with the same Android version (this will generate a warning but it works in most of the cases).

2. Generate a new device configuration that matches the device type and Android version of the device in question.

If you choose the second option, you can copy the configuration of an already working device and adopt the numbers in the XML file. These numbers represent the tables and columns of the noted database. To be a bit more precise, if you try to adopt the SMS database, you have to check the numbers for the following tables and columns:

```
<sms>
   <db_name>mmssms.db</db_name>
   <table_num>10</table_num>
   <sms_entry_positions>
      <id>0</id>
      <thread_id>1</thread_id>
      <address>2</address>
      <person>3</person>
      <date>4</date>
      <read>7</read>
      <type>9</type>
      <subject>11</subject>
      <body>12</body>
   </sms_entry_positions>
</sms>
```

The number for the table_num tag has to be set to the number that corresponds to the table called sms. The following numbers have to be adopted corresponding to the columns in the sms table that are named identically. The preceding printed example works with a Nexus 5 and Android 4.4.4. The same has to be done for all other databases too.

Running ADEL against a rooted Nexus 5 with Android 4.4.4 — filled with test data — generates the following output:

```
user@lab:~$./adel.py -d nexus5 -l 4
```

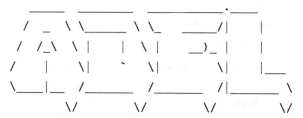

```
                Android Data Extractor Lite v3.0


ADEL MAIN:       ----> starting script....

ADEL MAIN:       ----> Trying to connect to smartphone or emulator....

dumpDBs:         ----> opening connection to device: 031c6277f0a6a117

dumpDBs:         ----> evidence directory 2015-07-20__22-53-22__031c6277f0a
6a117 created

ADEL MAIN:       ----> log file 2015-07-20__22-53-22__031c6277f0a6a117/log/
adel.log created

ADEL MAIN:       ----> log level: 4

dumpDBs:         ----> device is running Android OS 4.4.4

dumpDBs:         ----> dumping all SQLite databases....

dumpDBs:         ----> auto dict doesn't exist!

dumpDBs:         ----> weather database doesn't exist!

dumpDBs:         ----> weather widget doesn't exist!

dumpDBs:         ----> Google-Maps navigation history doesn't exist!

dumpDBs:         ----> Facebook database doesn't exist!

dumpDBs:         ----> Cached geopositions within browser don't exist!

dumpDBs:         ----> dumping pictures (internal_sdcard)....

dumpDBs:         ----> dumping pictures (external_sdcard)....

dumpDBs:         ----> dumping screen captures (internal_sdcard)....

dumpDBs:         ----> dumping screen captures (internal_sdcard)....

dumpDBs:         ----> all SQLite databases dumped

Screenlock:      ----> Screenlock Hash:
6a062b9b3452e366407181a1bf92ea73e9ed4c48
```

```
Screenlock:      ----> Screenlock Gesture: [0, 1, 2, 4, 6, 7, 8]

LocationInfo:    ----> Location map 2015-07-20__22-53-22__031c6277f0a6a117/
map.html created

analyzeDBs:      ----> starting to parse and analyze the databases....

parseDBs:        ----> starting to parse smartphone info

parseDBs:        ----> starting to parse calendar entries

parseDBs:        ----> starting to parse SMS messages

parseDBs:        ----> starting to parse call logs

parseDBs:        ----> starting to parse address book entries

analyzeDBs:      ----> all databases parsed and analyzed....

createReport:    ----> creating report....

ADEL MAIN:       ----> report 2015-07-20__22-53-22__031c6277f0a6a117/xml/
report.xml created

compareHash:     ----> starting to compare calculated hash values

ADEL MAIN:       ----> stopping script....


        (c) m.spreitzenbarth & s.schmitt 2015
```

In this output, you can see the name of the folder where all the data is dumped and where the generated report can be found. Additionally, you can also see the gesture of the screen lock that was automatically extracted and compared with a pre-generated rainbow table, as follows:

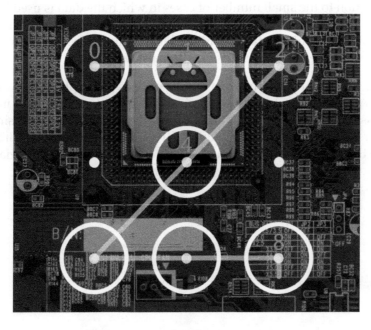

Movement profiles

In addition to data about individual communications, the *EU directive* from 2006 also requires certain location data to be retained by network operators. Specially, the directive requires that the following data is retained for at least six months:

- Identity and exact GPS coordinates of the radio cell where the user started a phone call

- Identity and coordinates of the radio cell that was active at the beginning of a GPRS data transmission

- Time stamps corresponding to this data

This information can help investigators to create movement profiles of suspects. Also, the information may be used to locate and monitor suspects.

Many EU member countries have implemented this directive in national laws. However, in some countries, there has been an intensive public debate about the laws, especially in relation to the threats to privacy. In Germany, the discussions were fueled by a dataset provided by the German politician Malte Spitz. The dataset contained location data over a period of six months that was preserved by his mobile network operator under the data retention law. A German newspaper created a graphical interface that enabled users to visually replay Spitz's detailed movements.

Overall, it is argued that retaining large amounts of data creates new risks of abuse. Also, the requirement to store data pertaining to millions of innocent people is out of proportion to the small number of cases in which the data is used by law enforcement. As a result, in 2011, the German Constitutional Court dismissed the original legislation requiring data retention. Meanwhile, the search for less invasive techniques to analyze the movements of criminals continues.

In the recent years, many new types of mobile phones (smartphones) have flooded the market. As they are essentially small personal computers, they offer much more than the possibility to make phone calls and surf the Internet. An increasing number of subscribers are using apps (mostly third-party applications that are directly installed on their phones) and communicating with friends and family via social networks such as Facebook, Google+, and Twitter.

For performance and other reasons, mobile devices persistently store location data in the local memory. In April 2011, it was reported that Android and iOS store sensitive geographical data. This data, which is maintained in system cache files, is regularly sent to platform developers. However, generating geographical data is not restricted to the operating system—many apps that provide location-based services also create and store such data. For example, Benford has shown that pictures taken by an iPhone contain the GPS coordinates of the location where the pictures were taken. Such data is sensitive because it can be used to create movement profiles as seen in the following figure. Unlike the location data that is retained by network operators, location data stored on smartphones can be accessed by law enforcement via an open seizure.

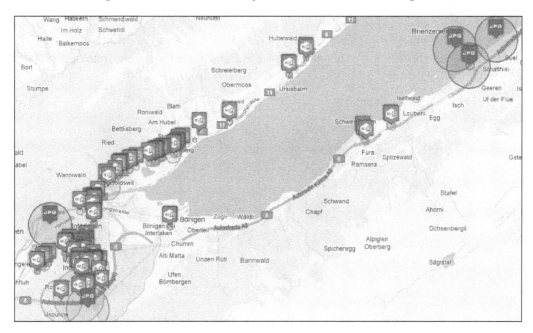

Apple iOS

After we have seen how to examine an Android-based smartphone, we now want to show you how to perform similar investigations on iOS-based devices. In the first section, we are using a **Secure Shell (SSH)** connection to the device and will show you how to get stored data from the keychain of a jailbroken iOS device.

In the second part of this section, we will use **libimobiledevice**. This library is a cross-platform library that uses the protocols to support iOS-based devices and allows you to easily access the device's filesystem, retrieve information about the device and it's internals, backup/restore the device, manage installed applications, retrieve PIM data as well as bookmarks, and so on. The most important fact is that the iOS-based device does not have to be jailbroken in order to be used — when dealing with libimobiledevice.

Getting the Keychain from a jailbroken iDevice

In many cases, it can be very helpful to get usernames and passwords of accounts that the user of the iDevice was using. This kind of data is located in the iOS keychain and can be pulled from iDevice with the help of the following script:

```python
import os, sys, subprocess


def get_kc(ip, backup_dir):

    # dumping the keychain
    print "Dumping the keychain ..."

    kc = subprocess.Popen(['scp', 'root@' + ip + ':/private/var/
Keychains/keychain-2.db', backup_dir],
        stdout=subprocess.PIPE, stdin=subprocess.PIPE,
stderr=subprocess.PIPE)
    kc.communicate()


def push_kcd(ip):

    # dumping the keychain
    print "Pushing the Keychain Dumper to the device ..."

    kcd = subprocess.Popen(['scp', 'keychain_dumper' 'root@' + ip +
':~/'],
        stdout=subprocess.PIPE, stdin=subprocess.PIPE,
stderr=subprocess.PIPE)
    kcd.communicate()


def exec_kcd(ip, backup_dir):
```

```
    # pretty print keychain
    kcc = subprocess.Popen(['ssh', 'root@' + ip, './keychain_dumper'],
        stdout=subprocess.PIPE, stdin=subprocess.PIPE,
stderr=subprocess.PIPE)
    kcc.communicate()
    kcc.stdout


if __name__ == '__main__':

    # starting to create the output directory
    backup_dir = sys.argv[1]

    try:
        os.stat(backup_dir)
    except:
        os.mkdir(backup_dir)

    # get the IP of the iDevice from user input
    ip = sys.argv[2]

    get_kc(ip, backup_dir)
    push_kcd(ip)
    exec_kcd(ip, backup_dir)
```

In the output of the preceding script, you can also find the password of the Apple account that the device is registered to:

```
Generic Password
----------------
Service: com.apple.account.AppleAccount.password
Account: 437C2D8F-****-****-****-************
Entitlement Group: apple
Label: (null)
Generic Field: (null)
Keychain Data: ************************
```

Manual Examination with libimobiledevice

This library uses common iOS protocols for communication between the investigator's machine and the connected iDevice. In order to work properly, the device has to be unlocked and paired because, otherwise a large amount of data on the device is still encrypted, and thus, protected.

With the help of the following script, you can create a full backup of the device (similar to an iTunes backup). Afterwards, the script will unpack the backup and print a hierarchical list of all files and folders in the backup. Dependent on the size of the iDevice this script can run for several minutes.

```python
import os, sys, subprocess


def get_device_info():

    # getting the udid of the connected device
    udid = subprocess.Popen(['idevice_id', '-l'], stdout=subprocess.
PIPE).stdout.readline().rstrip()

    print "connected device: \033[0;32m" + udid + "\033[m"
    return udid


def create_backup(backup_dir):

    # creating a backup of the connected device
    print "creating backup (this can take some time) ..."

    backup = subprocess.Popen(['idevicebackup2', 'backup', backup_
dir], stdout=subprocess.PIPE)
    backup.communicate()

    print "backup successfully created in ./" + backup_dir + "/"


def unback_backup(udid, backup_dir):

    # unpacking the backup
    print "unpacking the backup ..."

    backup = subprocess.Popen(['idevicebackup2', '-u', udid, 'unback',
backup_dir], stdout=subprocess.PIPE)
```

```
        backup.communicate()

        print "backup successfully unpacked and ready for analysis"


def get_content(backup_dir):

        # printing content of the created backup
        content = subprocess.Popen(['tree', backup_dir + '/_unback_/'],
stdout=subprocess.PIPE).stdout.read()
        f = open(backup_dir + '/filelist.txt', 'a+')
        f.write(content)
        f.close

        print "list of all files and folders of the backup are stored in
./" + backup_dir + "/filelist.txt"


if __name__ == '__main__':

        # check if device is connected
        if subprocess.Popen(['idevice_id', '-l'], stdout=subprocess.PIPE).
communicate(0)[0].split("\n")[0] == "":
                print "no device connected - exiting..."
                sys.exit(2)

        # starting to create the output directory
        backup_dir = sys.argv[1]

        try:
                os.stat(backup_dir)
        except:
                os.mkdir(backup_dir)

        udid = get_device_info()
        create_backup(backup_dir)
        unback_backup(udid, backup_dir)
        get_content(backup_dir)
```

The final output of this script will look like the following extract:

```
user@lab:~$ ./create_ios_backup.py out

connected device: 460683e351a265a7b9ea184b2802cf4fcd02526d
creating backup (this can take some time) ...
backup successfully created in ./out
unpacking the backup ...
backup successfully unpacked and ready for analysis
list of all files and folders of the backup are stored in ./out/filelist.
txt
```

With the help of the list of files and folders, you can start the analysis of the backup with common tools such as a plist file viewer or a SQLite browser. Searching for **Cydia App Store** in this generated file can also help to identify whether the smartphone has been jailbroken by the user or an attacker.

Summary

In this chapter, we covered the investigative process model from *Eoghan Casey* and adopted it to the case of smartphones. Later, we performed an analysis of Android smartphones in manual as well as automated ways with the help of Python scripts and the ADEL framework. In the last section, we covered the analysis of iOS-based smartphones.

After handling the forensic investigation of smartphones, we finished the physical and virtual acquisition and analysis and will shift the investigation to the volatile area of the devices in the next chapter.

7
Using Python for Memory Forensics

Now that you have performed investigations in the infrastructure (refer to *Chapter 4, Using Python for Network Forensics*), common IT equipment (refer to *Chapter 3, Using Python for Windows and Linux Forensics*), and even in the virtualized (refer to *Chapter 5, Using Python for Virtualization Forensics*) and mobile worlds (refer to *Chapter 6, Using Python for Mobile Forensics*), in this chapter, we will show you how to investigate in volatile memory with the help of Volatility, a Python-based forensics framework, on the following platforms:

- Android
- Linux

After showing you some basic Volatility plugins for Android and Linux and how to get the required RAM dump for analysis, we will go hunting for malware in RAM. Therefore, we will use YARA rules—based on pattern matching—and combine them with the power of Volatility.

Understanding Volatility basics

In general, memory forensics follow the same pattern as other forensic investigations:

1. Selecting the target of the investigation.
2. Acquiring forensic data.
3. Forensic analysis.

In the previous chapters, we already presented various technologies on how to select the target of an investigation, for example, starting from the system with unusual settings in the virtualization layer.

The acquisition of forensic data for memory analysis is highly dependent on the environment and we will discuss it in the *Using Volatility on Linux* and *Using Volatility on Android* sections of this chapter.

Always consider the virtualization layer as data source

Acquisition of memory from a running operating system always requires administrative access to this system and it is an intrusive process, that is, the process of data acquisition changes the memory data. Moreover, advanced malware is capable of manipulating the memory management of the operation system to prevent its acquisition. Therefore, always check and try to acquire the memory on the hypervisor layer as described in *Chapter 5, Using Python for Virtualization Forensics*.

The, by far, most prominent tool for the analysis of memory data is **Volatility**. Volatility is available at the Volatility Foundation on `http://www.volatilityfoundation.org/`.

The tool is written in Python and can be used free of charge under the terms of the GNU **General Public License (GPL)** version 2. Volatility is able to read memory dumps in various file formats, for example, hibernation files, raw memory dumps, VMware memory snapshot files, and the **Linux Memory Extractor (LiME)** format produced by the LiME module, which will be discussed later in this chapter.

The most important terms in the Volatility world are as follows:

- **Profile**: A profile helps Volatility in interpreting the memory offsets and structures of memory. The profile is dependent on the operating system, especially the OS kernel, machine, and CPU architecture. Volatility contains a variety of profiles for the most common use cases. In the *Using Volatility on Linux* section of this chapter, we will describe how to create your profiles.

- **Plugin**: Plugins are used to perform actions on the memory dump. Every Volatility command that you use calls a plugin to perform the corresponding action. For example, to get a list of all the processes that were running during the memory dump of a Linux system, the `linux_pslist` plugin is used.

Volatility provides a comprehensive documentation and we recommend that you get familiar with all the module descriptions to get the most usage out of Volatility.

Using Volatility on Android

To analyze volatile memory from Android devices, you will first need LiME. LiME is a **Loadable Kernel Module (LKM)** that gives access to the whole RAM of the device and can dump it to a physical SD card or network. After acquiring the volatile memory dump with LiME, we will show you how to install and configure Volatility to parse the RAM dump. In the last section, we will demonstrate how to get specific information out of the RAM dump.

LiME and the recovery image

LiME is a Loadable Kernel Module (LKM) that allows for volatile memory acquisition from Linux and Linux-based devices, such as Android. This makes LiME unique, as it is the first tool that allows for full memory captures on Android devices. It also minimizes its interaction between user and kernel space processes during acquisition, which allows it to produce memory captures that are more forensically sound than those of other tools designed for Linux memory acquisition.

In order to use LiME on Android, it has to be cross-compiled for the used kernel on the device in question. In the following sections, we will see how these steps are performed for a Nexus 4 with Android 4.4.4 (however, this approach can be adapted to every Android-based device for which the kernel—or at least the kernel configuration—is available as open source).

First of all, we have to install some additional packages on our lab system, as follows:

```
user@lab:~$ sudo apt-get install bison g++-multilib git gperf libxml2-
utils make python-networkx zlib1g-dev:i386 zip openjdk-7-jdk
```

After installing all the required packages, we now need to configure the access to USB devices. Under GNU/Linux systems, regular users directly can't access USB devices by default. The system needs to be configured to allow such access. This is done by creating a file named /etc/udev/rules.d/51-android.rules (as the root user) and inserting the following lines in it:

```
# adb protocol on passion (Nexus One)
SUBSYSTEM=="usb", ATTR{idVendor}=="18d1", ATTR{idProduct}=="4e12",
MODE="0600", OWNER="user"
# fastboot protocol on passion (Nexus One)
SUBSYSTEM=="usb", ATTR{idVendor}=="0bb4", ATTR{idProduct}=="0fff",
MODE="0600", OWNER="user"
# adb protocol on crespo/crespo4g (Nexus S)
SUBSYSTEM=="usb", ATTR{idVendor}=="18d1", ATTR{idProduct}=="4e22",
MODE="0600", OWNER="user"
# fastboot protocol on crespo/crespo4g (Nexus S)
```

```
SUBSYSTEM=="usb", ATTR{idVendor}=="18d1", ATTR{idProduct}=="4e20",
MODE="0600", OWNER="user"
# adb protocol on stingray/wingray (Xoom)
SUBSYSTEM=="usb", ATTR{idVendor}=="22b8", ATTR{idProduct}=="70a9",
MODE="0600", OWNER="user"
# fastboot protocol on stingray/wingray (Xoom)
SUBSYSTEM=="usb", ATTR{idVendor}=="18d1", ATTR{idProduct}=="708c",
MODE="0600", OWNER="user"
# adb protocol on maguro/toro (Galaxy Nexus)
SUBSYSTEM=="usb", ATTR{idVendor}=="04e8", ATTR{idProduct}=="6860",
MODE="0600", OWNER="user"
# fastboot protocol on maguro/toro (Galaxy Nexus)
SUBSYSTEM=="usb", ATTR{idVendor}=="18d1", ATTR{idProduct}=="4e30",
MODE="0600", OWNER="user"
# adb protocol on panda (PandaBoard)
SUBSYSTEM=="usb", ATTR{idVendor}=="0451", ATTR{idProduct}=="d101",
MODE="0600", OWNER="user"
# adb protocol on panda (PandaBoard ES)
SUBSYSTEM=="usb", ATTR{idVendor}=="18d1", ATTR{idProduct}=="d002",
MODE="0600", OWNER="user"
# fastboot protocol on panda (PandaBoard)
SUBSYSTEM=="usb", ATTR{idVendor}=="0451", ATTR{idProduct}=="d022",
MODE="0600", OWNER="user"
# usbboot protocol on panda (PandaBoard)
SUBSYSTEM=="usb", ATTR{idVendor}=="0451", ATTR{idProduct}=="d00f",
MODE="0600", OWNER="user"
# usbboot protocol on panda (PandaBoard ES)
SUBSYSTEM=="usb", ATTR{idVendor}=="0451", ATTR{idProduct}=="d010",
MODE="0600", OWNER="user"
# adb protocol on grouper/tilapia (Nexus 7)
SUBSYSTEM=="usb", ATTR{idVendor}=="18d1", ATTR{idProduct}=="4e42",
MODE="0600", OWNER="user"
# fastboot protocol on grouper/tilapia (Nexus 7)
SUBSYSTEM=="usb", ATTR{idVendor}=="18d1", ATTR{idProduct}=="4e40",
MODE="0600", OWNER="user"
# adb protocol on manta (Nexus 10)
SUBSYSTEM=="usb", ATTR{idVendor}=="18d1", ATTR{idProduct}=="4ee2",
MODE="0600", OWNER="user"
# fastboot protocol on manta (Nexus 10)
SUBSYSTEM=="usb", ATTR{idVendor}=="18d1", ATTR{idProduct}=="4ee0",
MODE="0600", OWNER="user"
```

Now the most time consuming part is coming—checking the source code of the Android version that is used. Depending on the speed of the hard drive and Internet connection, this step can take several hours so plan it in advance. Furthermore, keep it in mind that the source code is pretty big so use a second partition with at least 40 GB of free space. We install the source code for Android 4.4.4 as follows:

```
user@lab:~$ mkdir ~/bin
```

```
user@lab:~$ PATH=~/bin:$PATH
```

```
user@lab:~$ curl https://storage.googleapis.com/git-repo-downloads/repo >
~/bin/repo
```

```
user@lab:~$ chmod a+x ~/bin/repo
```

```
user@lab:~$ repo init -u https://android.googlesource.com/platform/
manifest -b android-4.4.4_r1
```

```
user@lab:~$ repo sync
```

After we have installed the source code for Android 4.4.4, we now need the sources for the kernel running on the device in question. For the Nexus 4 that we are using here, the right kernel is the **mako** kernel. A list of all available kernels for Google phones can be found at http://source.android.com/source/building-kernels.html.

```
user@lab:~$ git clone https://android.googlesource.com/device/lge/mako-
kernel/kernel
```

```
user@lab:~$ git clone https://android.googlesource.com/kernel/msm.git
```

Now that we have all the sources needed to cross-compile LiME, it is time to get LiME itself:

```
user@lab:~$ git clone https://github.com/504ensicsLabs/LiME.git
```

After cloning the git repository to our lab machine, now we have to set some environmental variables that are needed during the build process:

```
user@lab:~$ export SDK_PATH=/path/to/android-sdk-linux/
```

```
user@lab:~$ export NDK_PATH=/path/to/android-ndk/
```

```
user@lab:~$ export KSRC_PATH=/path/to/kernel-source/
```

```
user@lab:~$ export CC_PATH=$NDK_PATH/toolchains/arm-linux-
androideabi-4.9/prebuilt/linux-x86/bin/
```

```
user@lab:~$ export LIME_SRC=/path/to/lime/src
```

Next, we need to get the current kernel configuration from the device in question and copy it to the correct location in the LiME source. On our Nexus 4, this is possible by entering the following command:

```
user@lab:~$ adb pull /proc/config.gz
```

```
user@lab:~$ gunzip ./config.gz
```

```
user@lab:~$ cp config $KSRC_PATH/.config
```

```
user@lab:~$ cd $KSRC_PATH
```

```
user@lab:~$ make ARCH=arm CROSS_COMPILE=$CC_PATH/arm-eabi-modules_prepare
```

Before we can build the LiME kernel module, we need to write our customized Makefile:

```
obj-m := lime.o
lime-objs := main.o tcp.o disk.o
KDIR := /path/to/kernel-source
PWD := $(shell pwd)
CCPATH := /path/to/android-ndk/toolchains/arm-linux-androideabi-4.4.4/
prebuilt/linux-x86/bin/
default:
  $(MAKE) ARCH=arm CROSS_COMPILE=$(CCPATH)/arm-eabi- -C $(KDIR)
M=$(PWD) modules
```

With the help of this Makefile, we can build the kernel module that is needed to get the volatile memory from an Android device. Entering `make` can start this process.

In the following example, we will demonstrate how to push our newly generated kernel module to the device in question and dump the whole volatile memory to our lab environment through TCP.

If you have a device on which the kernel doesn't allow loading modules on the fly, you should consider creating your own recovery image (for example, a custom version of **TWRP** or **CWM**), include the LiME kernel module and flash it to the device in question. If you are fast enough during the flashing operation, there is nearly no data lost (for more information, refer to `https://www1.informatik.uni-erlangen.de/frost`).

The LiME module offers three different image formats that can be used to save a captured memory image on the disk: raw, padded, and lime. The third format—lime—is discussed in detail as it is our format of choice. The lime format has been especially developed to be used in conjunction with Volatility. It is supposed to allow easy analysis with Volatility and a special address space has been added to deal with this format. Every memory dump that is based on the lime format has a fixed size header, containing specific address space information for each memory range. This eliminates the need to have additional paddings just to fill up unmapped or memory mapped I/O regions. The LiME header specification is listed in the following:

```
typedef struct {
    unsigned int magic;          // Always 0x4C694D45 (LiME)
    unsigned int version;        // Header version number
    unsigned long long s_addr;   // Starting address of physical RAM
    unsigned long long e_addr;   // Ending address of physical RAM
    unsigned char reserved[8];   // Currently all zeros
} __attribute__ ((__packed__)) lime_mem_range_header;
```

To get such a dump from the Android device in question, connect to the Android device through `adb` and enter the following commands:

```
user@lab:~$ adb push lime.ko /sdcard/lime.ko
user@lab:~$ adb forward tcp:4444 tcp:4444
user@lab:~$ adb shell
nexus4:~$ su
nexus4:~$ insmod /sdcard/lime.ko "path=tcp:4444 format=lime"
```

On the lab machine, enter the following command to accept the data sent through TCP port 4444 from the Android device to the local lab machine:

```
user@lab:~$ nc localhost 4444 > nexus4_ram.lime
```

If the preceding commands are executed successfully, you will now have a RAM dump that can be further analyzed with the help of Volatility or other tools (refer to the next section).

Volatility for Android

After acquiring a dump file that represents the physical memory of the target system with the tools that we created in the previous section, we intend to extract data artifacts from it. Without an in-depth analysis of Android's memory structures, we would only be able to extract known file formats such as JPEG, or just the JPEG headers with the EXIF data (with tools such as **PhotoRec**) or simple ASCII strings, which are stored in a contiguous fashion (with common Linux tools such as **strings**) that could be used to brute force passwords on the devices in question. This approach is very limited as it can be used for any disk or memory dump but does not focus on OS and application-specific structures. As we intend to extract whole data objects from the Android system, we will make use of the popular forensic investigation framework for volatile memory: **Volatility**.

In this section, we will use a version of Volatility with ARM support (you need version 2.3 at least). Given a memory image, Volatility can extract running processes, open network sockets, memory maps for each process, and kernel modules.

Before a memory image can be analyzed, a Volatility profile must be created that is passed to the Volatility framework as a command line parameter. Such Volatility profile is a set of **vtype** definitions and optional symbol addresses that Volatility uses to locate sensitive information and parse it.

Basically, a profile is a compressed archive that contains two files, as follows:

- The `System.map` file contains symbol names and addresses of static data structures in the Linux kernel. In case of Android, this file is found in the kernel source tree after the kernel compilation.

- The `module.dwarf` file emerges on compiling a module against the target kernel and extracting the DWARF debugging information from it.

In order to create a `module.dwarf` file, a utility called `dwarfdump` is required. The Volatility source tree contains the `tools/linux` directory. If you run `make` in this directory, the command compiles the module and produces the desired DWARF file. Creating the actual profile is done by simply running the following command:

```
user@lab $ zip Nexus4.zip module.dwarf System.map
```

The resulting ZIP file needs to be copied to `volatility/plugins/overlays/linux`. After successfully copying the file, the profile shows up in the profiles section of the Volatility help output.

Although the support of Android in Volatility is quite new, there is a large amount of Linux plugins that are working perfectly on Android too. For example:

- `linux_pslist`: It enumerates all running processes of a system similar to the Linux ps command

- `linux_ifconfig`: This plugin simulates the Linux `ifconfig` command

- `linux_route_cache`: It reads and prints the route cache that stores the recently used routing entries in a hash table

- `linux_proc_maps`: This plugin acquires memory mappings of each individual process

If you are interested in how to write custom Volatility plugins and parse unknown structures in **Dalvik Virtual Machine** (**DVM**), please take a look at the following paper written by me and my colleagues: *Post-Mortem Memory Analysis of Cold-Booted Android Devices* (refer to `https://www1.informatik.uni-erlangen.de/filepool/publications/android.ram.analysis.pdf`).

In the next section, we will exemplarily show how to reconstruct the specific application data with the help of LiME and Volatility.

Reconstructing data for Android

Now, we will see how to reconstruct application data with the help of Volatility and custom made plugins. Therefore, we have chosen the call history and keyboard cache. If you are investigating on a common Linux or Windows system, there is already a large amount of plugins that are available, as you will see in the last section of this chapter. Unfortunately, on Android, you have to write your own plugins.

Call history

One of our goals is to recover the list of recent incoming and outgoing phone calls from an Android memory dump. This list is loaded when the phone app is opened. The responsible process for the phone app and call history is `com.android.contacts`. This process loads the `PhoneClassDetails.java` class file that models the data of all telephone calls in a history structure. One instance of this class is in memory per history entry. The data fields for each instance are typical meta information of a call, as follows:

- Type (incoming, outgoing, or missed)
- Duration
- Date and time

- Telephone number
- Contact name
- Assigned photo of the contact

To automatically extract and display this metadata, we provide a Volatility plugin called `dalvik_app_calllog`, which is shown as follows:

```
class dalvik_app_calllog(linux_common.AbstractLinuxCommand):

    def __init__(self, config, *args, **kwargs):
        linux_common.AbstractLinuxCommand.__init__(self, config,
*args, **kwargs)
        dalvik.register_option_PID(self._config)
        dalvik.register_option_GDVM_OFFSET(self._config)
        self._config.add_option('CLASS_OFFSET', short_option = 'c',
default = None,
        help = 'This is the offset (in hex) of system class
PhoneCallDetails.java', action = 'store', type = 'str')

    def calculate(self):
        # if no gDvm object offset was specified, use this one
        if not self._config.GDVM_OFFSET:
            self._config.GDVM_OFFSET = str(hex(0x41b0))

        # use linux_pslist plugin to find process address space and
ID if not specified
        proc_as = None
        tasks = linux_pslist.linux_pslist(self._config).calculate()
        for task in tasks:
            if str(task.comm) == "ndroid.contacts":
                proc_as = task.get_process_address_space()
                if not self._config.PID:
                    self._config.PID = str(task.pid)
                break

        # use dalvik_loaded_classes plugin to find class offset if
not specified
        if not self._config.CLASS_OFFSET:
            classes = dalvik_loaded_classes.dalvik_loaded_
classes(self._config).calculate()
            for task, clazz in classes:
```

```
                    if (dalvik.getString(clazz.sourceFile)+"" ==
"PhoneCallDetails.java"):
                        self._config.CLASS_OFFSET = str(hex(clazz.
obj_offset))
                    break

        # use dalvik_find_class_instance plugin to find a list of
possible class instances
        instances = dalvik_find_class_instance.dalvik_find_class_
instance(self._config).calculate()
        for sysClass, inst in instances:
            callDetailsObj = obj.Object('PhoneCallDetails', offset
= inst, vm = proc_as)
            # access type ID field for sanity check
            typeID = int(callDetailsObj.callTypes.contents0)
            # valid type ID must be 1,2 or 3
            if (typeID == 1 or typeID == 2 or typeID == 3):
                yield callDetailsObj

    def render_text(self, outfd, data):
        self.table_header(outfd, [    ("InstanceClass", "13"),
                                    ("Date", "19"),
                                    ("Contact", "20"),
                                    ("Number", "15"),
                                    ("Duration", "13"),
                                    ("Iso", "3"),
                                    ("Geocode", "15"),
                                    ("Type", "8")
                                    ])
        for callDetailsObj in data:
            # convert epoch time to human readable date and time
            rawDate = callDetailsObj.date / 1000
            date =    str(time.gmtime(rawDate).tm_mday) + "." + \
                      str(time.gmtime(rawDate).tm_mon) + "." + \
                      str(time.gmtime(rawDate).tm_year) + " " + \
                      str(time.gmtime(rawDate).tm_hour) + ":" + \
                      str(time.gmtime(rawDate).tm_min) + ":" + \
                      str(time.gmtime(rawDate).tm_sec)

            # convert duration from seconds to hh:mm:ss format
            duration =    str(callDetailsObj.duration / 3600) + "h
" + \
```

```
                                    str((callDetailsObj.duration % 3600) /
60) + "min " + \
                                    str(callDetailsObj.duration % 60) + "s"

                    # replace call type ID by string
                    callType = int(callDetailsObj.callTypes.contents0)
                    if callType == 1:
                        callType = "incoming"
                    elif callType == 2:
                        callType = "outgoing"
                    elif callType == 3:
                        callType = "missed"
                    else:
                        callType = "unknown"

                    self.table_row(     outfd,
                                        hex(callDetailsObj.obj_offset),
                                        date,
                                        dalvik.parseJavaLangString(callDeta
ilsObj.name.dereference_as('StringObject')),
                                        dalvik.parseJavaLangString(callDeta
ilsObj.formattedNumber.dereference_as('StringObject')),
                                        duration,
                                        dalvik.parseJavaLangString(callDeta
ilsObj.countryIso.dereference_as('StringObject')),
                                        dalvik.parseJavaLangString(callDeta
ilsObj.geoCode.dereference_as('StringObject')),
                                        callType)
```

This plugin accepts the following command line parameters:

- -o: For an offset to the gDvm object
- -p: For a process ID (PID)
- -c: For an offset to the PhoneClassDetails class

If some of these parameters are known and passed on to the plugin, the runtime of the plugin reduces significantly. Otherwise, the plugin has to search for these values in RAM itself.

Keyboard cache

Now, we want to have a look at the cache of the default keyboard application. Assuming that no further inputs were given after unlocking the screen and the smartphone is protected by a PIN, this PIN is equal to the last user input, which can be found in an Android memory dump as a UTF-16 Unicode string. The Unicode string of the last user input is created by the `RichInputConnection` class in the `com.android.inputmethod.latin` process and is stored in a variable called `mCommittedTextBeforeComposingText`. This variable is like a keyboard buffer, that is, it stores the last typed and confirmed key strokes of the on-screen keyboard. To recover the last user input, we provide a Volatility plugin called `dalvik_app_lastInput`, as follows:

```
class dalvik_app_lastInput(linux_common.AbstractLinuxCommand):

    def __init__(self, config, *args, **kwargs):
        linux_common.AbstractLinuxCommand.__init__(self, config,
*args, **kwargs)
        dalvik.register_option_PID(self._config)
        dalvik.register_option_GDVM_OFFSET(self._config)
        self._config.add_option('CLASS_OFFSET', short_option = 'c',
default = None,
        help = 'This is the offset (in hex) of system class
RichInputConnection.java', action = 'store', type = 'str')

    def calculate(self):

        # if no gDvm object offset was specified, use this one
        if not self._config.GDVM_OFFSET:
            self._config.GDVM_OFFSET = str(0x41b0)

        # use linux_pslist plugin to find process address space and
ID if not specified
        proc_as = None
        tasks = linux_pslist.linux_pslist(self._config).calculate()
        for task in tasks:
            if str(task.comm) == "putmethod.latin":
                proc_as = task.get_process_address_space()
                self._config.PID = str(task.pid)
                break

        # use dalvik_loaded_classes plugin to find class offset if
not specified
        if not self._config.CLASS_OFFSET:
```

```
            classes = dalvik_loaded_classes.dalvik_loaded_
classes(self._config).calculate()
                for task, clazz in classes:
                        if (dalvik.getString(clazz.sourceFile)+"" ==
"RichInputConnection.java"):
                                self._config.CLASS_OFFSET = str(hex(clazz.
obj_offset))
                                break

            # use dalvik_find_class_instance plugin to find a list of
possible class instances
            instance = dalvik_find_class_instance.dalvik_find_class_
instance(self._config).calculate()
                for sysClass, inst in instance:
                    # get stringBuilder object
                    stringBuilder = inst.clazz.getJValuebyName(inst,
"mCommittedTextBeforeComposingText").Object.dereference_as('Object')
                    # get superclass object
                    abstractStringBuilder = stringBuilder.clazz.super.
dereference_as('ClassObject')

                    # array object of super class
                    charArray = abstractStringBuilder.
getJValuebyName(stringBuilder, "value").Object.dereference_
as('ArrayObject')
                    # get length of array object
                    count = charArray.length
                    # create string object with content of the array object
                    text = obj.Object('String', offset = charArray.
contents0.obj_offset,
                        vm = abstractStringBuilder.obj_vm, length = count*2,
encoding = "utf16")
                    yield inst, text

    def render_text(self, outfd, data):
        self.table_header(outfd, [    ("InstanceClass", "13"),
                                      ("lastInput", "20")
                                      ])

        for inst, text in data:

            self.table_row(    outfd,
                               hex(inst.obj_offset),
                               text)
```

Actually, this plugin not only recovers PINs but also arbitrary user inputs that were given last; this might be an interesting artifact of digital evidence in many cases. Similar to the preceding plugin, it accepts the same three command line parameters: `gDvm offset`, `PID`, and `class file offset`. If none, or only some, of these parameters are given, the plugin can also automatically determine the missing values.

Using Volatility on Linux

In the following section, we will describe memory acquisition techniques and sample use cases to use Volatility for Linux memory forensics.

Memory acquisition

If the system is not virtualized and therefore, there is no way of getting the memory directly from the hypervisor layer; then even for Linux, our tool of choice is LiME.

However, unlike in Android, the tool installation and operation is a lot easier because we generate and run LiME directly on Linux system; however, many steps are quite similar as you will notice in the following paragraphs.

First, determine the exact kernel version, which is running on the system, that is to be analyzed. If there is no sufficient documentation available, then you may run the following command to get the kernel version:

```
user@forensic-target $ uname -a
Linux forensic-target 3.2.0-88-generic #126-Ubuntu SMP Mon Jul 6 21:33:03
UTC 2015 x86_64 x86_64 x86_64 GNU/Linux
```

Use the configuration management in enterprise environments

Enterprise environments often run configuration management systems that show you the kernel version and Linux distribution of your target system. Asking your customer to provide you with this data or even a system with an identical kernel version and software environment can help you in reducing the risk of incompatibilities between the LiME module and your forensic target.

In your lab environment, prepare the LiME kernel module for memory acquisition. To compile the module, make sure you have the correct kernel source code version available for your target and then issue the following build command in the `src` directory of LiME:

```
user@lab src $ make -C /usr/src/linux-headers-3.2.0-88-generic M=$PWD
```

This should create the `lime.ko` module in the current directory.

On the target system, this kernel module can be used to dump the memory to disk, as follows:

```
user@forensic-target $ sudo insmod lime.ko path=/path/to/dump.lime
format=lime
```

We recommend choosing a path on the network to write the image to. This way, the changes made to the local system are minimal. Transferring the image over network is also an option. Just follow the description in the *Using Volatility on Android* section.

Volatility for Linux

Volatility comes with a wide range of *profiles*. These profiles are used by Volatility to interpret the memory dump. Unfortunately, the wide variety of Linux kernels, system architectures, and kernel configurations make it impossible to ship the profiles to all versions of Linux kernels.

Listing all the profiles of Volatility

The list of all available profiles can be retrieved with the `vol.py --info` command.

Consequently, it may be necessary to create your own profile as an ideal match to the forensic target. The Volatility framework supports this step by providing a dummy module that must be compiled against the kernel headers of the target system. This module is available in the Volatility distribution in the `tools/linux` subdirectory. Compile it— similar to LiME— but with debug settings enabled:

```
user@lab src $ make -C /usr/src/linux-headers-3.2.0-88-generic CONFIG_
DEBUG_INFO=y M=$PWD
```

This creates `module.ko`. There is no need to load this module; all we need is its debug information. We use the `dwarfdump` tool, which is available as an installation package in most Linux distributions, to extract this debug information:

```
user@lab $ dwarfdump -di module.ko > module.dwarf
```

The next step in the creation of our profile is to acquire the `System.map` file of the target system or a system with identical architecture, kernel version, and kernel configuration. The `System.map` file may be found in the `/boot` directory. Often, the kernel version is included in the filename, therefore be sure to select the `System.map` file for the running kernel of the forensic target system.

Put `module.dwarf` and `System.map` into a zip archive, which will become our Volatility profile, as shown in the following:

```
user@lab $ zip Ubuntu3.2.0-88.zip module.dwarf System.map
```

As shown in the example, the name of the ZIP file should reflect the distribution and kernel version.

 Make sure that you do not add additional path information to the zip archive. Otherwise, Volatility may fail to load the profile data.

Copy the new profile to the Linux profile directory of Volatility, as follows:

```
user@lab $ sudo cp Ubuntu3.2.0-88.zip /usr/local/lib/python2.7/dist-
packages/volatility-2.4-py2.7.egg/volatility/plugins/overlays/linux/
```

Instead of using the system-wide profile directory, you may also choose a new one and add the `--plugins=/path/to/profiles` option to your Volatility command line.

Finally, you need to get the name of your new profile for further use. Therefore, use the following call:

```
user@lab $ vol.py --info
```

The output should contain one additional line showing the new profile, as shown in the following:

```
Profiles
--------

LinuxUbuntu3_2_0-88x64 - A Profile for Linux Ubuntu3.2.0-88 x64
```

To use this profile, add `--profile=LinuxUbuntu3_2_0-88x64` as the command line argument for all subsequent calls to `vol.py`.

Reconstructing data for Linux

All plugins that analyze Linux memory dumps have the `linux_` prefix. Therefore, you should use the Linux version of the plugins. Otherwise, you may get an error message notifying that the module is not supported in the selected profile.

Analyzing processes and modules

A typical first step in the analysis of a memory dump is to list all running processes and loaded kernel modules.

The following is how to carve out all running processes from a memory dump with Volatility:

```
user@lab $ vol.py --profile=LinuxUbuntu3_2_0-88x64 --file=memDump.lime
linux_pslist

Volatility Foundation Volatility Framework 2.4
```

Offset	Name	Pid	Uid	
Gid	DTB	Start Time		
-----------------	--------------------	---------------	---------------	
------	-----------------	----------		
0xffff8802320e8000	init	1	0	0
0x000000022f6c0000	2015-08-16 09:51:21 UTC+0000			
0xffff8802320e9700	kthreadd	2	0	0
-----------------	2015-08-16 09:51:21 UTC+0000			
0xffff88022fbc0000	cron	2500	0	0
0x000000022cd38000	2015-08-16 09:51:25 UTC+0000			
0xffff88022fbc1700	atd	2501	0	0
0x000000022fe28000	2015-08-16 09:51:25 UTC+0000			
0xffff88022f012e00	irqbalance	2520	0	0
0x000000022df39000	2015-08-16 09:51:25 UTC+0000			
0xffff8802314b5c00	whoopsie	2524	105	
114	0x000000022f1b0000	2015-08-16 09:51:25 UTC+0000		
0xffff88022c5c0000	freshclam	2598	119	
131	0x0000000231fa7000	2015-08-16 09:51:25 UTC+0000		

As shown in the output, the `linux_pslist` plugin iterates the kernel structure by describing active processes, that is, it starts from the `init_task` symbol and iterates the `task_struct->tasks` linked list. The plugin gets a list of all running processes, including their offset address in the memory, process name, process ID (PID), numerical ID of the user and group of the process (UID, and GID), and start time. The **Directory Table Base (DTB)** can be used in the further analysis to translate physical into virtual addresses. Empty DTB entries relate, most likely, to a kernel thread. For example, `kthreadd` in our example output.

Analyzing networking information

The memory dump contains various information about the network activity of our forensic target system. The following examples show how to utilize Volatility to derive the information about the recent network activity.

The **Address Resolution Protocol (ARP) cache** of the Linux kernel maps MAC addresses to IP addresses. Before a network communication on the *local network* is established, the Linux kernel sends an ARP request to get the information about the corresponding MAC address for a given destination IP address. The response is cached in memory for re-use to further communicate with this IP address on the local network. Consequently, ARP cache entries indicate the systems on the local network that the forensic target was communicating with.

To read the ARP cache from a Linux memory dump, use the following command:

```
user@lab $ vol.py --profile=LinuxUbuntu3_2_0-88x64 --file=memDump.lime
linux_arp
[192.168.167.22                              ] at 00:00:00:00:00:00    on
eth0
[192.168.167.20                              ] at b8:27:eb:01:c2:8f    on
eth0
```

This extract from the output shows that the system had a cache entry for the `192.168.167.20` destination address with `b8:27:eb:01:c2:8f` being the corresponding MAC address. The first entry is most likely a cache entry that results from an unsuccessful communication attempt, that is, the `192.168.167.22` communication partner did not send a response to an ARP request that was transmitted from the system and therefore, the corresponding ARP cache entry remained at its initial value of `00:00:00:00:00:00`. Either the communication partner was not reachable or it is simply nonexistent.

If large parts of your local subnet show up in the ARP cache with multiple entries having a MAC address of 00:00:00:00:00:00, then this is an indicator of the scanning activity, that is, the system has tried to detect other systems on the local network.

For further network analysis, it might be worth checking the list of MAC addresses that are retrieved from the ARP cache against the systems that are supposed to be on the local subnet. While this technique is not bulletproof (as MAC addresses can be forged), it might help in discovering rogue network devices.

 Looking up the hardware vendor for a MAC address

The prefix of a MAC address reveals the hardware vendor of the corresponding network hardware. Sites such as `http://www.macvendorlookup.com` provide an indication of the hardware vendor of a network card.

If we look up the hardware vendor for the `b8:27:eb:01:c2:8f` MAC address from our example, it shows that this device was manufactured by the Raspberry Pi Foundation. In a standard office or data center environment, these embedded devices are rarely used and it is definitely worth checking whether this device is benign.

To get an overview of the network activity at the time the memory dump was created, Volatility provides the means to emulate the `linux_netstat` command, as follows:

```
user@lab $ vol.py --profile=LinuxUbuntu3_2_0-88x64 --file=memDump.lime
linux_netstat
TCP      192.168.167.21  :55622 109.234.207.112  :  143 ESTABLISHED
thunderbird/3746
UNIX 25129           thunderbird/3746
TCP      0.0.0.0         : 7802 0.0.0.0          :    0 LISTEN
skype/3833
```

These three lines are only a small excerpt from the typical output of this command. The first line shows that the `thunderbird` process with the `3746` PID has an active `ESTABLISHED` network connection to the IMAP server (TCP port `143`) with the `109.234.207.112` IP address. The second line merely shows a socket of UNIX type that is used for **Inter-Process Communication (IPC)**. The last entry shows that `skype` with the `3833` PID is a waiting `LISTEN` for incoming connections on TCP port `7802`.

Volatility can also be used to narrow down the list of processes to those with raw network access. Typically, this kind of access is only required for **Dynamic Host Configuration Protocol (DHCP)** clients, network diagnostics, and, of course, malware in order to construct arbitrary packets on the network interface, for example, conduct a so-called ARP cache poisoning attack. The following shows how to list the processes with raw network sockets:

```
user@lab $ vol.py --profile=LinuxUbuntu3_2_0-88x64 --file=memDump.lime
linux_list_raw

Process          PID     File Descriptor Inode

---------------- ------  --------------- -------------------

dhclient         2817                  5               15831
```

Here, only the DHCP client is detected to have the raw network access.

Rootkit detection modules

Volatility provides a variety of mechanisms in order to detect typical rootkit behavior, for example, interrupt hooking, manipulations of the network stack, and hidden kernel modules. We recommend getting familiar with these modules as they can speed up your analysis. Furthermore, check for module updates on a regular basis to leverage new malware detection mechanisms being built in to Volatility.

Some generic methods and heuristics for malware detection are combined in the `linux_malfind` module. This module looks for suspicious process memory mappings and produces a list of possibly malicious processes.

Malware hunting with the help of YARA

YARA itself is a tool that is able to match a given pattern in arbitrary files and datasets. The corresponding rules — also known as signatures — are a great way to search for known malicious files in dumps of hard drives or memory.

In this section, we want to demonstrate how to search for given malware in an acquired memory dump of a Linux machine. Therefore, you can use two different procedures that we will discuss in the following:

- Searching the memory dump directly with the help of YARA
- Using `linux_yarascan` and Volatility

The first option has one big disadvantage; as we already know, memory dumps contain fragmented data that is normally contiguous. This fact makes it prone to failure if you are searching this dump for known signatures as they are not necessarily in the order you are searching them.

The second option — using `linux_yarascan` — is more fail-safe as it uses Volatility and knows the structure of the acquired memory dump. With the help of this knowledge, it is able to resolve the fragmentation and search reliable for known signatures. Although, we are using `linux_yarascan` on Linux, this module is also available for Windows (`yarascan`) and Mac OS X (`mac_yarascan`).

The main capabilities of this module are as follows:

- Scan given processes in the memory dump for a given YARA signature
- Scan the complete range of kernel memory
- Extract the memory areas to disk that contain positive results to the given YARA rules

The full list of possible command line options can be seen on entering `vol.py linux_yarascan -h`

Basically, you can search in many different ways. The simplest way of using this module is by searching for a given URL in the memory dump. This can be done by entering the following command:

```
user@lab $ vol.py --profile=LinuxUbuntu3_2_0-88x64 --file=memDump.lime
linux_yarascan --yara-rules="microsoft.com" --wide


Task: skype pid 3833 rule r1 addr 0xe2be751f

0xe2be751f   6d 00 69 00 63 00 72 00 6f 00 73 00 6f 00 66 00
m.i.c.r.o.s.o.f.

0xe2be752f   74 00 2e 00 63 00 6f 00 6d 00 2f 00 74 00 79 00
t...c.o.m./.t.y.

0xe2be753f   70 00 6f 00 67 00 72 00 61 00 70 00 68 00 79 00
p.o.g.r.a.p.h.y.

0xe2be754f   2f 00 66 00 6f 00 6e 00 74 00 73 00 2f 00 59 00
/.f.o.n.t.s./.Y.

0xe2be755f   6f 00 75 00 20 00 6d 00 61 00 79 00 20 00 75 00
o.u...m.a.y...u.

0xe2be756f   73 00 65 00 20 00 74 00 68 00 69 00 73 00 20 00
s.e...t.h.i.s...

0xe2be757f   66 00 6f 00 6e 00 74 00 20 00 61 00 73 00 20 00
f.o.n.t...a.s...
```

```
0xe2be758f   70 00 65 00 72 00 6d 00 69 00 74 00 74 00 65 00
p.e.r.m.i.t.t.e.

0xe2be759f   64 00 20 00 62 00 79 00 20 00 74 00 68 00 65 00
d...b.y...t.h.e.

0xe2be75af   20 00 45 00 55 00 4c 00 41 00 20 00 66 00 6f 00
..E.U.L.A...f.o.

0xe2be75bf   72 00 20 00 74 00 68 00 65 00 20 00 70 00 72 00
r...t.h.e...p.r.

0xe2be75cf   6f 00 64 00 75 00 63 00 74 00 20 00 69 00 6e 00
o.d.u.c.t...i.n.

0xe2be75df   20 00 77 00 68 00 69 00 63 00 68 00 20 00 74 00
..w.h.i.c.h...t.

0xe2be75ef   68 00 69 00 73 00 20 00 66 00 6f 00 6e 00 74 00
h.i.s...f.o.n.t.

0xe2be75ff   20 00 69 00 73 00 20 00 69 00 6e 00 63 00 6c 00
..i.s...i.n.c.l.

0xe2be760f   75 00 64 00 65 00 64 00 20 00 74 00 6f 00 20 00
u.d.e.d...t.o...
```

Task: skype pid 3833 rule r1 addr 0xedfe1267

```
0xedfe1267   6d 00 69 00 63 00 72 00 6f 00 73 00 6f 00 66 00
m.i.c.r.o.s.o.f.

0xedfe1277   74 00 2e 00 63 00 6f 00 6d 00 2f 00 74 00 79 00
t...c.o.m./.t.y.

0xedfe1287   70 00 6f 00 67 00 72 00 61 00 70 00 68 00 79 00
p.o.g.r.a.p.h.y.

0xedfe1297   2f 00 66 00 6f 00 6e 00 74 00 73 00 2f 00 59 00
/.f.o.n.t.s./.Y.

0xedfe12a7   6f 00 75 00 20 00 6d 00 61 00 79 00 20 00 75 00
o.u...m.a.y...u.

0xedfe12b7   73 00 65 00 20 00 74 00 68 00 69 00 73 00 20 00
s.e...t.h.i.s...

0xedfe12c7   66 00 6f 00 6e 00 74 00 20 00 61 00 73 00 20 00
f.o.n.t...a.s...

0xedfe12d7   70 00 65 00 72 00 6d 00 69 00 74 00 74 00 65 00
p.e.r.m.i.t.t.e.

0xedfe12e7   64 00 20 00 62 00 79 00 20 00 74 00 68 00 65 00
d...b.y...t.h.e.

0xedfe12f7   20 00 45 00 55 00 4c 00 41 00 20 00 66 00 6f 00
..E.U.L.A...f.o.

0xedfe1307   72 00 20 00 74 00 68 00 65 00 20 00 70 00 72 00
r...t.h.e...p.r.
```

```
0xedfe1317   6f 00 64 00 75 00 63 00 74 00 20 00 69 00 6e 00
o.d.u.c.t...i.n.

0xedfe1327   20 00 77 00 68 00 69 00 63 00 68 00 20 00 74 00
..w.h.i.c.h...t.

0xedfe1337   68 00 69 00 73 00 20 00 66 00 6f 00 6e 00 74 00
h.i.s...f.o.n.t.

0xedfe1347   20 00 69 00 73 00 20 00 69 00 6e 00 63 00 6c 00
..i.s...i.n.c.l.

0xedfe1357   75 00 64 00 65 00 64 00 20 00 74 00 6f 00 20 00
u.d.e.d...t.o...
```

A more complex but also a more realistic way is to search for a given YARA rule. The following YARA rule was made to identify whether a system has been infected with the `Derusbi` malware family:

```
rule APT_Derusbi_Gen
{
meta:
   author = "ThreatConnect Intelligence Research Team"
strings:
   $2 = "273ce6-b29f-90d618c0" wide ascii
   $A = "Ace123dx" fullword wide ascii
   $A1 = "Ace123dx1!" fullword wide ascii
   $A2 = "Ace123dx!@#x" fullword wide ascii
   $C = "/Catelog/login1.asp" wide ascii
   $DF = "~DFTMP$$$$.1" wide ascii
   $G = "GET /Query.asp?loginid=" wide ascii
   $L = "LoadConfigFromReg failded" wide ascii
   $L1 = "LoadConfigFromBuildin success" wide ascii
   $ph = "/photoe/photo.asp HTTP" wide ascii
   $PO = "POST /photos/photo.asp" wide ascii
   $PC = "PCC_IDENT" wide ascii
condition:
   any of them
}
```

If we save this rule as `apt_derusbi_gen.rule`, we can search for it in the acquired memory dump by entering the following command:

```
user@lab $ vol.py --profile=LinuxUbuntu3_2_0-88x64 --file=memDump.lime
linux_yarascan --yara-file=apt_derusbi_gen.rule --wide
```

The result will only show us a short preview that can be enlarged by using the `--size` option.

If you are investigating a predefined scenario (for example, if you already know that the system has been attacked by a known group), you can copy all your rules in one single rule file and search the memory dump for all the rules in the file at once. Volatility and `linux_yarascan` will display every hit and its corresponding rule number. This makes it much faster to scan for known malicious behavior in a memory dump.

There is a vast number of sources for YARA signatures that are available in the wild and we will only mention some of the most important ones here to help you, starting with the malware hunt as shown in the following:

- The YARA signature exchange group on Google Groups: `http://www.deependresearch.org/`

- Signatures from AlienVault Labs: `https://github.com/AlienVault-Labs/AlienVaultLabs/tree/master/malware_analysis`

- Antivirus signatures that can be built with the help of ClamAV and recipe 3-3 out of the Malware Analyst's Cookbook: `https://code.google.com/p/malwarecookbook/source/browse/trunk/3/3/clamav_to_yara.py`

Summary

In this chapter, we provided an overview of memory forensics using the Volatility framework. In the examples, we demonstrated memory acquisition techniques for Android and Linux systems and saw how to use LiME on both systems. We used Volatility to get information about running processes, loaded modules, possibly malicious activity, and recent network activity. The latter is useful to trace the activities of an attacker through the network.

In the last example in this chapter, we demonstrated how to search for a given malware signature or other highly flexible pattern-based rules in such a memory dump. These YARA signatures or rules help in identifying suspicious activities or files really fast.

Furthermore, we demonstrated how to get the keyboard cache as well as call history from an Android device.

Where to go from here

If you like to test the tools and knowledge gained from this book, we have the following two tips for you:

- Create a lab with two virtual machines—**Metasploit** and **Metasploitable**. Try to hack into your **Metasploitable** system and perform a forensic analysis afterwards. Are you able to reconstruct the attack and gather all the Indicators of Compromise?

- Get some old hard drives, which are no longer used but have been used regularly in the past. Perform a forensic analysis on these drives and try to reconstruct as much data as possible. Are you able to reconstruct former operations on these drives?

If you like to enhance your knowledge on some of the topics that were covered in this book, the following books are a really good choice:

- *Practical Mobile Forensics* by *Satish Bommisetty, Rohit Tamma, Heather Mahalik, Packt Publishing*

- *The Art of Memory Forensics: Detecting Malware and Threats in Windows, Linux, and Mac Memory* by *Michael Hale Ligh, Andrew Case, Jamie Levy* and *AAron Walters, Wiley India*

- *Handbook of Digital Forensics and Investigation* by *Eoghan Casey, Academic Press*

Index

A

Address Resolution Protocol (ARP) **83, 157**
algorithms
  about 11, 12
  MD5 12, 13
  SHA256 13
  SSDEEP 13, 14
Android
  automated examination, with ADEL 126
  examining 115
  manual examination 115-125
  movement profiles, creating 132, 133
Android Data Extractor Lite (ADEL)
  about 112
  design guidelines 126
  implementation 127, 128
  system workflow 127, 128
  URL 128
  working with 128-131
Android Software Development Kit
  (Android SDK) 127
AndroTotal 119
AppExtract
  about 20
  URL 20
Apple iOS
  about 134
  keychain, obtaining from jailbroken
    iDevice 134, 135
  manual examination, with
    libimobiledevice 136-138
Application Compatibility Shim Cache 43

atom
  about 3
  URL 3

B

bare-metal hypervisor 86

C

capability flags 53
C data types 6, 7
central log system
  log information, collecting 91
clustering, file information
  about 66
  histograms, creating 66-70
Context Triggered Piecewise Hashing
  (CTPH) 14
cryptographic hash function
  about 11
  properties 12
ctypes
  about 1, 4, 5
  C data types 6, 7
  Dynamic Link Libraries (DLL) 5
  Structures, defining 8, 9
  Unions, defining 8, 9
Cyber Security 1
Cydia App Store 138

D

Dalvik Virtual Machine (DVM) 147
Data center as a Service (DCaaS) 96

Python virtual environment. *See* virtualenv
pyVmomi
  about 88
  sample code 88
  URL 88

R

RAM content
  forensic copies, creating 105, 106
real-world scenarios
  Mobile Malware 19
  NSRLquery 19, 23
recovery image
  creating 141-145
regular expression
  about 50
  re module 50
rip-smb-uploads decoder 80
rogue machines
  creating 88-90
rogue network interfaces
  detecting 96-101

S

Scapy
  about 77
  URL 81
  using 81-83
scikit-learn
  about 71
  URL 71
sdb 15
Secure Shell (SSH) 133
Server Message Block (SMB) 77
SHA256 11-13
shared objects (SO) 5
Shim Cache Parser
  about 40, 43, 44
  reference link 40
  URL 43
smartphones
  Investigative Process Model 112
smart pointer 65

snapshots
  about 87
  using, as disk images 107
SSDEEP
  about 11-14
  URL 14
stat module
  reference link 55
strings 146
Structures
  defining 8, 9

T

Tor2Web service 80
Tor network 80
Tor Onion Services 80
Type 1 hypervisor 86
Type 2 hypervisor 86

U

Ubuntu
  setting up 2, 3
  URL 2
Unions
  defining 8, 9

V

Vawtrak malware 80
vCenter Server 87
virtualenv
  about 2, 3
  installing 3
  setting up 3, 4
virtualization
  as additional layer of abstraction 86-88
  as new attack surface 85
  forensic copies, creating of
    RAM content 105, 106
  network traffic, capturing 108
  rogue machines, creating 88-90
  snapshots, using as disk images 107
  systems, cloning 91-96
  used, as source of evidence 105

Thank you for buying
Mastering Python Forensics

About Packt Publishing

Packt, pronounced 'packed', published its first book, *Mastering phpMyAdmin for Effective MySQL Management*, in April 2004, and subsequently continued to specialize in publishing highly focused books on specific technologies and solutions.

Our books and publications share the experiences of your fellow IT professionals in adapting and customizing today's systems, applications, and frameworks. Our solution-based books give you the knowledge and power to customize the software and technologies you're using to get the job done. Packt books are more specific and less general than the IT books you have seen in the past. Our unique business model allows us to bring you more focused information, giving you more of what you need to know, and less of what you don't.

Packt is a modern yet unique publishing company that focuses on producing quality, cutting-edge books for communities of developers, administrators, and newbies alike. For more information, please visit our website at www.packtpub.com.

About Packt Open Source

In 2010, Packt launched two new brands, Packt Open Source and Packt Enterprise, in order to continue its focus on specialization. This book is part of the Packt Open Source brand, home to books published on software built around open source licenses, and offering information to anybody from advanced developers to budding web designers. The Open Source brand also runs Packt's Open Source Royalty Scheme, by which Packt gives a royalty to each open source project about whose software a book is sold.

Writing for Packt

We welcome all inquiries from people who are interested in authoring. Book proposals should be sent to author@packtpub.com. If your book idea is still at an early stage and you would like to discuss it first before writing a formal book proposal, then please contact us; one of our commissioning editors will get in touch with you.

We're not just looking for published authors; if you have strong technical skills but no writing experience, our experienced editors can help you develop a writing career, or simply get some additional reward for your expertise.

Big Data Forensics – Learning Hadoop Investigations

ISBN: 978-1-78528-810-4   Paperback: 264 pages

Perform forensic investigations on Hadoop clusters with cutting-edge tools and techniques

1. Identify, collect, and analyze Hadoop evidence forensically.

2. Learn about Hadoop's internals and Big Data file storage concepts.

3. A step-by-step guide to help you perform forensic analysis using freely available tools.

Python for Secret Agents

ISBN: 978-1-78398-042-0   Paperback: 216 pages

Analyze, encrypt, and uncover intelligence data using Python, the essential tool for all aspiring secret agents

1. Build a toolbox of Python gadgets for password recovery, currency conversion, and civic data hacking.

2. Use steganography to hide secret messages in images.

3. Get to grips with geocoding to find villains' secret lairs.

Please check **www.PacktPub.com** for information on our titles